The Genius of
Opposites

Other books by the author

The Introverted Leader

Quiet Influence

The Genius of
Opposites

How Introverts and Extroverts Achieve Extraordinary Results Together

Jennifer B. Kahnweiler, PhD

BK

Berrett–Koehler Publishers, Inc.
a BK Business book

Berrett-Koehler Publishers, Inc.
235 Montgomery Street, Suite 650
San Francisco, CA 94104-2916
Tel: (415) 288-0260 Fax: (415) 362-2512 www.bkconnection.com

Ordering Information

Quantity sales. Special discounts are available on quantity purchases by corporations, associations, and others. For details, contact the "Special Sales Department" at the Berrett-Koehler address above.

Individual sales. Berrett-Koehler publications are available through most bookstores. They can also be ordered directly from Berrett-Koehler: Tel: (800) 929-2929; Fax: (802) 864-7626; www.bkconnection.com

Orders for college textbook/course adoption use. Please contact Berrett-Koehler: Tel: (800) 929-2929; Fax: (802) 864-7626.

Orders by U.S. trade bookstores and wholesalers. Please contact Ingram Publisher Services, Tel: (800) 509-4887; Fax: (800) 838-1149; E-mail: customer.service@ingrampublisherservices.com; or visit www.ingrampublisherservices.com/Ordering for details about electronic ordering.

Berrett-Koehler and the BK logo are registered trademarks of Berrett-Koehler Publishers, Inc.

Printed in the United States of America

Berrett-Koehler books are printed on long-lasting acid-free paper. When it is available, we choose paper that has been manufactured by environmentally responsible processes. These may include using trees grown in sustainable forests, incorporating recycled paper, minimizing chlorine in bleaching, or recycling the energy produced at the paper mill.

Library of Congress Cataloging-in-Publication Data
Kahnweiler, Jennifer B.
The genius of opposites : how introverts and extroverts achieve
    extraordinary results together / by Jennifer B. Kahnweiler. -- First edition.
    pages cm
    Includes bibliographical references and index.
    ISBN 978 1-62656-305-6 (pbk.)
    1. Interpersonal conflict. 2. Interpersonal relations. 3. Introversion.
    4. Extroversion. 5. Conflict management. 6. Psychology, Industrial. I. Title.
    BF637.I48K34 2015
    158.2--dc23
                                                                    2015015345

First Edition
20 19 18 17 16 15   10 9 8 7 6 5 4 3 2 1

Interior design and project management: Dovetail Publishing Services
Cover design: Ian Koviak / The Book Designers

To my daughters, Lindsey and Jessie,
who open my heart

Contents

Preface

"It comes down to different styles. That is the cause of most conflicts at work. You are an extrovert, Jennifer, and Amy, your assistant, is an introvert. Until you accept that basic fact and learn to work with her, your department won't get to where it needs to be."

These words from Peter, an outside company consultant, were hard to hear. I had really worked at moving Amy along and expected her to adopt my energy and pace. None of my efforts were working. Trying to fix Amy and mold her into a "mini-Jennifer" was actually making things worse. Our partnership had already fizzled despite my herculean efforts.

Though it was too late to make things work then, failing to establish a productive work relationship with Amy did motivate me to learn more about introverts and extroverts. This book is the result of my extensive research with many famous and not so famous introvert/extrovert duos over a thirty-year consulting, coaching, and speaking career.

You will discover why it can be so hard to thrive in some of your relationships with opposites. You will learn about five essential steps that successful opposites use to navigate the tricky waters of their relationships. And you will discover why these five steps are important, how they can break down, and what practical solutions you can use to achieve extraordinary results together.

What's in This Book?

Because I rarely read a book cover to cover myself, I've tried to make the book easy to navigate—and include short summaries and questions for you to consider at the end of each chapter. That way you can dip in and out of chapters that interest you.

We start off in the introduction with the major theme of the book: opposites are most successful when they stop focusing on their differences and use approaches that move them toward results.

In Chapter 1, "Who Are These Unlikely Duos?," you will learn about the strengths and friction points for introverts and extroverts when they work together. Chapter 2, "How to Mix Oil and Water," lays out the Genius of Opposites Process, the basis of the book. You will learn how both you and your opposite can "Accept the Alien," "Bring on the Battles," "Cast the Character," "Destroy the Dislike," and learn why "Each Can't Offer Everything." There is a quiz to help you assess what you have in common with high-functioning opposites. You can take it and compare your results with your partner's results.

Chapters 3 through 7 are replete with stories of genius opposites in workplaces around the world. You will learn from their experiences what to do and not to do when handling the dynamic act of working together.

Chapter 8 wraps it all up and helps you jumpstart your plan for success.

So are you ready to hear about:

- The world-famous composers who felt they had much more to offer the world in an already-impressive roster of songs, but they couldn't get over their dislike of each other?

- The automobile CEO who was outmaneuvered by a new CEO in an ill-fated "merger of equals"?

- The remarkably insightful pair of film critics who almost missed their chance to appreciate each other's great gifts because they were so busy competing with each other?

- The skilled consultants who lost their business because they couldn't reconcile their styles and modify their firm when the Great Recession hit?

Given that an estimated approximately 50 percent of people in the world fall on either the introvert or extrovert side of the spectrum, chances are that you have interacted with or will interact with your opposites often. The outcomes of some of your wildly successful and disastrous ventures were determined by whether you were in synch with or at polarity from introverts or extroverts. Perhaps you've left a project because one of the key team members was an opposite type to you, and the frustration overcame you.

There is no way to assess how many breakthrough ideas never broke through because opposites could not get over the barriers their differences caused. You may have a few in mind from your own career.

It doesn't have to be that way. . . .

Introduction

A Deceptively Easy but Highly Delicate Balancing Act

Introvert and extrovert opposites, working together, can accomplish great things. Think John Lennon and Paul McCartney, Sheryl Sandberg and Mark Zuckerberg, Steve Jobs and Steve Wozniak, Ralph David Abernathy and Martin Luther King Jr., and Eleanor Roosevelt and Franklin Roosevelt. The list is extensive—likely in your life as well.

Opposites like these attract, right? They often get along very well as work partners and fill in each other's voids. They create beautiful harmonies together.

Yet, there is another pervasive and darker truth. These high-performing duos may have the illusion of being effortlessly well balanced. In reality, complementary opposites can go off the rails very quickly, and the damage can be as negative as the impacts are positive.

There are often temporary and longer deep freezes and estrangements between partners. Advice columnists and twin sisters Ann Landers and Abigail Van Buren didn't speak for seven years. Politicians Teddy Roosevelt and William Howard Taft let politics overtake their friendship. The

Nobel prize–winning scientists James Watson and Francis Crick stopped working together after they discovered DNA. We are familiar with the pain of too many of these work and personal breakups between opposites.

Think of marriage as one example of this phenomenon. For a marriage to succeed, we need to figure out how to deal with each other beyond the initial attraction and honeymoon phases. We know that both partners need to work at it. A happy marriage doesn't just happen.

The truth is that these opposite pairs require constant vigilance, careful maintenance, and balance. Without this focused attention, not only do the partners experience frustration, but their potentially great contributions are not realized. In the workplace, their organizations, clients, and customers all lose out.

So what is the common theme of success?

The key is to remember that these relationships are most successful when opposites stop focusing on their differences and use approaches that move them toward results.

Why Now Is the Time for
The Genius of Opposites

"You Know Who Is Missing Here?"

For years, I have trained and coached introverts about how to find their leadership voice and make a difference. Every time I lead a seminar, introverts tell me, "You know who is missing here, Jennifer? My boss, my spouse, my co-worker! They need to hear that nothing is wrong with us and that we have so many strengths to offer. I don't hate extroverts; in fact, I have a child who is one. I do like their outgoing ways, but I am not sure how to get a word in edgewise!"

We often judge each other. Introverts see extroverts as speaking before thinking, using too many words to express themselves, being poor listeners, and appearing self-centered. Introverts know how extroverts get irritated with them because of their slower pace and more measured tones, and are puzzled and frustrated about how to manage the energy and expressive nature of their extroverted work colleagues.

Extroverts turn out to be just as frustrated with introverts. They see introverts as slow to respond, unemotional, and dismissive of their own achievements. They don't understand the introvert's need for quiet time and can be frustrated by a more measured response that requires them to "pull teeth" to get a quick answer.

Extroverts also understand that the outward energy they view as a strength is often too much for their quieter colleagues to handle. They are also clueless about how to dial it down. To them, the introverts' quiet robs the organization of potential ideas and innovations.

Opposites Can Produce Exponential Results

Until now, there has not been a process to blend the complementary talents of introverts and extroverts. But the remarkable thing is that when you skillfully combine the extrovert set of strengths with those of the introvert, you don't just get addition. You get exponential results.

It's like having one group who can see only close up and one who can see only in the distance. When you bring them together and manage the blend, the entire picture comes into focus and suddenly you can act on things the way neither side could have separately. The possibilities for these two styles collaborating are great for those individuals, but also for their workplaces, including improved morale, surpassed company goals, and the high that comes from satisfying work.

Partnerships Are the New Work Model

The individualistic, self-centered career path is shifting toward one of more collaboration. This new model of work includes former competitors coming together as working partners, sellers collaborating with their customers, and global partners joining across continents to achieve their goals. If these are to blossom, opposites need to understand a key dimension of personality style—introversion and extroversion—and use this knowledge to strengthen themselves and their partnership.

So How Can We Really Make This I/E Thing Work?

Since the publication of my last two books, *The Introverted Leader* and *Quiet Influence*, along with *Quiet* by Susan Cain and other titles, the topic of introversion has touched a deep recognizable nerve. The rise of the introverts is a real movement. I have heard from hundreds of readers about how they finally feel validated. Large and small organizations are taking introversion more seriously and even recognizing it as an important element of diversity. An increasing demand for training and speaking programs is evidence of this shift, as well as the creation of quiet office spaces to accommodate introverts' needs.

This book is built upon the shoulders of the hundreds of introverts and extroverts who have opened up to me over a ten-year period. Through hundreds of conversations during and after my presentations and in numerous dialogues with my online community, people have asked about how to get along with the "other half." "How do we as introverts and extroverts achieve great results together?" they ask. How can we really make it work? This groundswell of interest told me now is the time to discover the elements of this delicate balance. It is the next natural step.

Glide Seamlessly in and out of Conversations

The sooner that introverts and extroverts learn about each other's different languages, the quicker they can get to results. We work together in offices, on conference calls, and through text messages. Yet it often feels like we introverts and extroverts are speaking entirely different languages. We need to learn how to glide more seamlessly in and out of these conversations with as little stress as possible.

Being able to do this not only gets results but is also personally gratifying. Olivia, an extroverted corporate trainer, works closely with introverts. She said of her introverted colleague and friend Henry, "It is not a competition for the spotlight. Henry is my biggest fan. He sees my strengths when I don't see them." Henry said, "Olivia has her antenna up and is cued into others' needs. We pass the baton to each other and don't care who has the fun part."

What My Research Discovered About Opposites

To understand and eventually surface the necessary protons and electrons of the Genius of Opposites model, I interviewed more than forty introvert and extrovert partners. The interviewees represent different career fields, genders, ages, nationalities, and organizations. I first gave them a set of questions about the dynamics of working with their opposite, and they opened up to me about their learnings and the highs and lows of navigating a relationship with their opposite.

The Genius of Opposites Has a Five-Step ABCDE Process

In this latest research, I culled their key lessons and themes and boiled down their secret sauce into five key steps. I then placed these steps into an easy to remember five-step ABCDE process. You will read about how the Genius of Opposites Process works and even be able to take a quiz to determine how close you are to achieving "genius status."

As you read this book and hear the stories of others, I hope you will discover the power of working with a current opposite and the many other opposites you interact with regularly at work. I anticipate that you will awaken your own genius by using the five steps that have launched other pairs into the sheer enjoyment of creating together something they could not have produced alone.

Who Is This Book For?

This book is for introverts and extroverts working in organizations across the globe who who are in partnerships within and outside their diverse organizations. These are not limited to internal partnerships, but also include those with outside customers, suppliers, and strategic partners. In addition, coaches, trainers, and managers who want to bring out the best in their employees will benefit from the ideas and solutions presented here.

So here is a sneak preview of the process.

The Genius of Opposites Process

Each of these steps is an essential component of a strong partnership.

1. **Accept the Alien**: You can't change your opposite, but you can understand them. Once you are able to accept this fact, you are in for much less stress.

2. **Bring on the Battles**: See disagreement as necessary to arriving at better outcomes because you challenge each other to come up with better solutions together than you would alone.

3. **Cast the Character**: Know each person's role in a scenario and cast them so that you bring out

your opposite's best. Opposites share the credit no matter what role they take.

4. **Destroy the Dislike**: When you respect each other and act like friends, you can talk openly and have fun.

5. **Each Can't Offer Everything**: Know that each one of you is incapable of offering everything, so for true diversity, you work in concert to provide the widest range of options to others.

Figure I.1 The ABCs of The Genius of Opposites Process

Accept the Alien
Bring on the Battles
Cast the Character
Destroy the Dislike
Each Can't Offer Everything

Summary: Preventing the Crash and Burn

The benefits such relationships bring are self-evident, but there's also a price to pay when they are not properly maintained. For every success story about two opposites who made it work, there are four or five about opposites who crashed and burned because they couldn't reconcile their different styles.

If you and your opposite are already thriving, this book is your maintenance manual, your key to avoiding the crash and burn. If you're just embarking on an opposites relationship, this book can stop you both from going terribly and off track. Then it will become your maintenance manual. Proceed with respect and caution: genius opposites do not just "happen."

Part I

The Basics

Chapter 1

Who Are These Unlikely Duos?

One going up, one coming down
But we seem to land on common ground
When things go wrong we make corrections
To keep things moving in the right direction
Try to fight it but I'm telling you, Jack,
It's useless, opposites attract.

Oliver Leiber, Songwriter for Paula Abdul[1]

What Are Genius Opposites?

Genius opposites are partnerships made up of introverts and extroverts in all types of combinations. These include executives and admins, creatives and their collaborators, sales people and office support personnel, project managers and their sponsors, and more.

These powerful teams have a unique chemistry and achieve outcomes they never could achieve alone. But they take work to succeed, and the magic rises from their differences. Although their styles are divergent, the results of their collaboration look like they came from a single mind. *Their relationships are most successful when they stop focusing on their differences and use approaches that move them toward results.*

Be Sure You're Defining Introverts and Extroverts Accurately

Introverts get their energy from within, and extroverts get theirs from the outside world. Though many of us claim to fall somewhere in the middle on this energy scale, we do tend to lean one way or another.

You can also behave more extroverted or introverted in a specific situation. For example, as an extrovert, you may be very comfortable at large holiday parties with strangers, but you may clam up with the finance team, with whom you have less confidence. Or as an introvert, you may speak powerfully in a prepared talk but be tongue-tied with your co-workers at lunch.

The deal-breaker question of whether you are more of an introvert or extrovert is this: Do you need time to recharge after being with people? If the answer is a resounding yes!, then there is a good chance you are an introvert. But if it is just a medium yes, then you are likely more extroverted. While that distinction may not be especially scientific, it is practical.

Beth Buelow is an expert on introverted entrepreneurs and author of *The Introvert Entrepreneur*.[2] In complimenting an introvert/extrovert pair who made their business work as opposites, Beth said, "You are mastering being together together."[3] That mastery describes many of the partners you will meet in this book. In different ways, they are seeking to deliver results together. You will also read about the breakdowns that occur along the way between introverts and extroverts, and how to avoid them. Here are a few of the problems that can occur as a result of introvert/extrovert differences. Can you identify with any of these in either your work or personal life?

Opposite Wiring Causes Misfiring

The people who drive us crazy often view the world through different lenses. In fact, those "lens" differences or traits that we at first find endearing often become the ones we can't stand. I loved my introverted husband Bill's quiet, calm demeanor when we were dating. A year later, I found those long pauses irritating. *Why doesn't he answer when I ask a question?* I thought. The truth was that Bill was responding in the same slow cadence as before, but the honeymoon was over and I was less accepting. He still expresses himself that way more than forty years later. Fortunately, learning about introvert/extrovert preferences helped me to reframe his long pauses and accept his need to think first before he spoke.

In addition to differences in pace of speech, these natural differences can also lead to conflict between introverts and extroverts.

Wiring Challenge #1: Being Alone Versus with People

Introverts need and want to spend time alone. They prefer quiet, private spaces and like to handle projects individually, one on one, or in small groups. Extroverts have a hard time understanding that and often feel the need to intrude on that solitude. My husband Bill, in his humorous way, has a large "Do Not Disturb" sign on his door, as a fifteen-year-old boy might! Extroverts need a strong signal like that to know introverts mean business when they say they need alone time.

Writer Jonathan Rauch explains, "Extroverts . . . assume that company, especially their own, is always welcome. . . . As often as I have tried to explain the matter to extroverts, I have never sensed that any of them really understood. They listen for a moment and then go back to barking and yipping."[4]

Extroverts thrive on being out among people, love meeting new ones and packing a lot into a day. The more activities the better it is. When extrovert Steve Cohn, a director of learning, is on the road, he likes to eat with his colleagues, to "hear sixteen conversations going on at the same time." An introverted team member told him that at the end of the day, she had given everything she had while in the classroom and needed to recharge. She headed up to her room and that was it for the evening. Cohn was irritated at first, but changed his thinking when he thought about it. He explained, "I teach this stuff (communication skills), so I am understanding."

Until partners understand these differences, they may not be as understanding and resent team members who don't join in evening socializing. Being alone or being with people can create challenges in customer interactions as well. Introverts are challenged when they are thrust into gatherings designed for networking with strangers. Extroverts are frustrated when a customer or client squelches their rapport-building time by being uncommunicative or wanting to get to business.

Wiring Challenge #2: Thinking It Through Versus Talking It Out

Introverts need space and time to process their thoughts. Even in casual conversations, they consider others' comments carefully. They stop and reflect before responding and know how to use the power of the pause to let everyone's words sink in. Extroverts are impatient while waiting for introverts to finish their thoughts. They also express frustration about having to ask questions in order to pull ideas from their introverted counterparts, especially when decisions must be made. They often are ready to move while their introvert partners are still pondering the options.

Extroverts may not have fully formed their ideas, but are forming them aloud as they speak. Introverts find this tiring and become confused trying to follow an extrovert's running commentary. They may even think that the extrovert has changed his mind when he is expressing a new thought; actually, the thought was just percolating aloud. Consultant and author Emily Axelrod illustrates the point: "It used to frustrate Dick (her husband and business partner) when I would think out loud. Once, I ran to him and said, 'Let's go to the movies. We can see this, this, this, or this!' He just looked at me. Suddenly, it dawned on me: it frustrated him when I would talk about all these things that we could do because he thought we had to do them all!'"

Wiring Challenge #3: Being Private Versus Being an Open Book

Introverts keep personal matters under wraps, sharing information with only a select few. Even then, they share it only after they know people well and feel a high level of comfort with them. Extroverts want to connect and warm up to people more quickly. They may perceive introverts as standoffish, aloof, and downright angry when first meeting them, especially when introverts don't quickly self-disclose. Introverts, on the other hand, find the questions and immediate best-friend camaraderie intrusive.

That extroverts need to talk, talk, and talk to everyone often baffles the introvert. Author and leadership consultant Devora Zack tells introverts in her classes that extroverts say, "I can talk to anyone about anything." She has watched those same introverts "stare with mouths dropped open, as if upon their first viewing of a UFO."[5]

Summary: Figure Out the Wiring

The new model of work requires that we collaborate and understand how extroverts and introverts are wired differently. Not understanding how these different wires can cross can cause serious damage in being productive, satisfied, and ultimately in serving your customers.

Your natural disposition toward or away from solitude, your preference for thinking or talking aloud and being private or an open book are all potential causes for disagreement. Though their styles are divergent and these unlikely duos take work to succeed, the magic rises from their differences. The results of their collaboration look like they came from a single mind.

Chapter 2

How to Mix Oil and Water—The Genius of Opposites Process and Quiz

Are you ready to move toward extraordinary results with your opposite? As tempting as it may seem to fix them first, your first step is to look at yourself. Take stock of how you see the dynamics of your partnership playing out. What is working, and what needs some adjusting from your perspective? Ideally, your opposite is also willing to take an honest assessment and feels motivated like you to move toward a new genius level of performance.

One way to assess your partnership and to begin to move toward that new level of performance is to take this short quiz. It's designed to help you evaluate how well you interact with your partner and perform on the job using the five steps discussed in Chapter 1 of this book.

The Quiz

Use the quiz as a way to assess your progress as you apply the ideas in the book. Based on the characteristics that set genius opposites apart, you will learn what you have in common with highly effective opposites.

Directions

If you are an introvert, envision your interaction with a work colleague who is an extrovert. When answering the following questions as an extrovert, envision your interaction with a work colleague who is an introvert. If you are not sure or feel you are closely tied between the two, review chapter 1 for some clues.

Assess yourself by indicating how often you engage in these behaviors, using a scale from 1 (never) to 5 (almost always).

Rating Guidelines

Your initial response is usually the most valid, so don't second guess yourself. Also avoid being too tough or easy a critic on yourself. If you were an objective outside rater, how would you grade yourself on these five key steps using the scale below?

Accept the Alien					
1. I am able to read my opposite's non-verbal signals.	**1** Never	**2** Rarely	**3** Sometimes	**4** Often	**5** Almost Always
2. I am patient with my opposite's different approaches.	**1** Never	**2** Rarely	**3** Some times	**4** Often	**5** Almost Always
3. We give each other updates and communicate on a regular basis.	**1** Never	**2** Rarely	**3** Sometimes	**4** Often	**5** Almost Always
4. We have developed a shorthand for communicating.	**1** Never	**2** Rarely	**3** Sometimes	**4** Often	**5** Almost Always

	1	2	3	4	5
5. I have accepted that I cannot change my opposite.	Never	Rarely	Some-times	Often	Almost Always
Bring on the Battles					
6. I regularly challenge my opposite's thinking.	Never	Rarely	Some-times	Often	Almost Always
7. I keep my partner's energy preference in mind during conflict.	Never	Rarely	Some-times	Often	Almost Always
8. We take time-outs when we need time to recharge.	Never	Rarely	Some-times	Often	Almost Always
9. We keep our eye on our shared vision.	Never	Rarely	Some-times	Often	Almost Always
10. We are open to bringing in a third party to break through an impasse.	Never	Rarely	Some-times	Often	Almost Always
Cast the Character					
11. We discuss who should take what role before each engagement.	Never	Rarely	Some-times	Often	Almost Always
12. We share equal credit on projects.	Never	Rarely	Some-times	Often	Almost Always
13. I advocate for my opposite as needed.	Never	Rarely	Some-times	Often	Almost Always
14. At times, we break out of our expected roles.	Never	Rarely	Some-times	Often	Almost Always
15. We provide feedback to each other on a regular basis.	Never	Rarely	Some-times	Often	Almost Always

Destroy the Dislike					
16. On most days, I am on friendly terms with my partner.	**1** Never	**2** Rarely	**3** Some-times	**4** Often	**5** Almost Always
17. We balance the need for privacy and sharing information.	**1** Never	**2** Rarely	**3** Some-times	**4** Often	**5** Almost Always
18. We are able to laugh with each other in a good-natured way.	**1** Never	**2** Rarely	**3** Some-times	**4** Often	**5** Almost Always
19. We are inspired by common values.	**1** Never	**2** Rarely	**3** Some-times	**4** Often	**5** Almost Always
20. I see short term friendships with opposites as a chance to learn.	**1** Never	**2** Rarely	**3** Some-times	**4** Often	**5** Almost Always
Each Can't Offer Everything					
21. Clients tell us they benefit from our diverse and divergent opinions.	**1** Never	**2** Rarely	**3** Some-times	**4** Often	**5** Almost Always
22. We gather information on what is and isn't working with our clients.	**1** Never	**2** Rarely	**3** Some-times	**4** Often	**5** Almost Always
23. We are clear about our own ideas and positions before meeting with customers.	**1** Never	**2** Rarely	**3** Some-times	**4** Often	**5** Almost Always
24. My partner and I model openness to our clients.	**1** Never	**2** Rarely	**3** Some-times	**4** Often	**5** Almost Always
25. We take steps to understand our clients' introverted and extroverted energy.	**1** Never	**2** Rarely	**3** Some-times	**4** Often	**5** Almost Always

How to Score and Interpret the Quiz

Take these steps to get the most out of the Genius of Opposites quiz:

1. Grab a piece of paper or a note-taking app on your phone.

2. Total the numbers you circled on the quiz. This is your score.

3. Review the description of your score in the table on the next page and consider the suggestions in the scoring table to enhance your individual performance.

4. Use these results as a way to gauge what you are doing effectively. Consider them a starting point. You can focus on steps of the Genius of Opposites Process that are relevant to you and collect solutions while reading.

5. Encourage your partner to take the quiz and discuss your responses. Did you differ in your overall scores? What about in the categories? Were there any questions that you viewed completely differently?

6. Decide to work on one area either individually or together. You are moving toward extraordinary results by opening up this important dialogue.

Score Range	Score Description and Suggestions
113–125	**Very Strong** You are using many of the strengths of highly effective genius opposites. Look at how you can apply your strengths to take this partnership to an even higher level and consider how you can improve other opposite partnerships.
100–112	**Solid** You are doing well in demonstrating genius opposite strengths. Some areas still could use some attention. Pinpoint the times when your efforts to partner are not successful. See if you recognize any differences between your use of the five steps in successful and unsuccessful situations.
75–99	**Moderate** You have some work to do in ramping up your Genius of Opposites behavior. Look at a work situation where you are not being effective and consider which different steps you can add to your mix. Discuss solutions with your partner and try them on.
74 and below	**Lots of Room for Improvement** You have some work to do in living up to your Genius of Opposites potential. Start by noticing your own behavior and asking your partner and others for honest feedback and suggestions. Begin by working on one step that you want to develop and set a specific goal for this week. Check in with your partner as you make changes.

The Genius of Opposites Process

Now that you have an idea of the areas you excel in and those to enhance, use this summary to keep these steps top of mind as you venture forth in the book. We will be exploring each step in the process throughout the next five chapters. Pay particular attention to the solutions at

Figure 2.1 The ABCs of The Genius of Opposites Process

Accept the Alien
Bring on the Battles
Cast the Character
Destroy the Dislike
Each Can't Offer Everything

the end each of those five chapters for ideas that you and your opposite can immediately apply

Potential Areas of Genius Performance for Opposites

1. **Accept the Alien**: You can't change your opposite, but you can understand them. Once you are able to accept this fact, you are in for much less stress.

2. **Bring on the Battles**: See disagreement as necessary to arrive at better outcomes because you challenge each other to come up with better solutions.

3. **Cast the Character**: Know each person's role in a scenario and cast him or her so that you bring out your opposite's best in that role. Opposites share the credit no matter what role they take.

4. **Destroy the Dislike**: When you respect each other and act like friends, you can talk openly and have fun.

5. **Each Can't Offer Everything**: Know that each one of you is incapable of offering everything and that for true diversity you must work in concert to provide the widest range of options to others.

Summary: Use Your Findings from the Quiz to Move to the Next Level

To move toward extraordinary results with your opposite, take stock of yourself and your partnership by completing the Genius of Opposites quiz. Review your scores to determine what you want to build on and what you want to change and keep it close by as you read the book, collecting solutions along the way. Encourage your opposite to take the quiz. Use the quiz as a starting point for discussion. Then consider the five steps of the Genius of Opposites Process, review the solutions at the end of Chapters 3 through 7, and decide what changes you will immediately make to achieve extraordinary results.

Part II
The Steps

Chapter 3

Accept the Alien

"Accept that your partner is a pain in the ass. Accept that you are a pain in the ass, so the two of you are made for each other. Accept that what makes you furious about your partner is wrapped up with what excites you. What you most love and what drives you crazy is the same thing. Just on a bad hair day."[6]

—Joshua Wolf Shenk, author of *Powers of Two*

Accept the Alien: You can't change your opposite, but you can understand them. Once you are able to accept this fact, you are in for much less stress.

Anthony Morris and Errol la Grange run a growing online training organization in Melbourne, Australia. These opposites' creative ideas explode like popcorn.

Anthony is a thoughtful and mild-mannered introvert who sent me fully thought-out responses to my questions about their partnership. Errol is a smiling extrovert who shows up in daily Facebook posts, meeting people around the world. He thrives on going to coffee shops and chatting with just about anyone. Their complementary differences showed up when I met them both for the first time. Anthony wore what he called his "good ole brown pull-on shoes" purchased from a local shoe store, and Errol stood out in his turquoise cowboy boots from San Francisco, making for a great conversation starter.

Both partners thrive on innovation and keep growing their global business, taking advantage of technology to find the best way to deliver learning solutions to their clients. They are leaders in the Massive Online Open Classroom (MOOC) movement, leading global initiatives in this new emerging field.

Their deep mutual affection and respect spring from having built a business and friendship together over the past ten years. Anthony smiles knowingly at his partner, and Errol pauses to allow Anthony space to interject his thoughts.

Errol also describes how talking through conflict deepens their strong partnership. "We often have different perspectives on strategy. We talk it through and usually come to better solutions together than alone. We understand that conflict holds the key to opportunity at its core. There is also a lot of intuitive guidance in how we relate." They "can often sense what the other is feeling," says Errol. There are times when one of them feels particularly strongly and the other goes along with the idea.

They disagree, but there is no doubt that these two get past the friction of their natural disappointments. They accept the alien and that helps them get things done.

Why Accepting the Alien Matters

Communication is such a loaded word. The dictionary definition is vanilla: the exchange of information between two people. But we all know that exchange can carry misunderstanding, friction, and annoyance. When introvert/extrovert partnerships are rocky, the conflict usually reflects a breakdown in this exchange. Sometimes the person sitting across from you with all those weird interpretations of what the client said can feel as alien to you as something that crawled out of a spaceship. When that happens, stifle the impulse to flee or grab a weapon. Genius beckons.

In describing those inevitable times, introvert/extrovert partners will say, "It is too much work to figure him/ her out." Or they will avoid their opposite, leading to a pile of unattended hurts, disconnects, and confusion that are difficult to come back from.

Successful introvert/extrovert opposites make the decision to accept each other and not let communication differences impede their ultimate outcome: to make a great product, deliver the best service possible, and achieve breakthroughs.

There are two key reasons why accepting the alien matters: it builds empathy and makes the partnership stronger.

Acceptance Builds Empathy in Each Partner

Maybe you have participated in a "blind walk" exercise designed to awaken understanding for the visually impaired. I recall being led blindfolded down a wooded trail. I relied on my partner John's every step, afraid I would stumble and fall without his guidance. I also noticed how my other senses kicked in—smell, hearing, and touch ready to help guide me along.

After that experience, I had a glimmer of awareness of what it might be like to experience blindness. I also realized the opportunities to awaken other parts of my brain even though I could never truly know what it is like to fully inhabit a blind person's experience.

It is the same with introvert/extrovert relationships. When we work with our opposite, we have great opportunities to appreciate another view, even though we don't understand everything they live through. But by stepping into their world, we also awaken parts of ourselves that have lain dormant, allowing us to throttle up our performance. Suddenly, the person doesn't seem like an alien after all.

The Partnership Becomes Stronger

Through the process of working closely together, opposites can become a stronger unit over time. When they face successes and failures, both have grown together, not just individually. An exponential power forms to help them meet the next challenge, the next opportunity.

When we grapple with tough problems and decisions together, not only do we learn more about how to move forward as a team, but also more opportunities to be creative emerge.

In the entertainment business, rejection and disappointments are as daily as coffee and bagels. Referring to his 1971 musical *Follies* collaborator James Goldman, Stephen Sondheim observed, "One of the advantages of having a collaborator is that you are never slammed in the face alone. You are always in the boat with somebody."[7]

Good communication with your partner allows you to collaborate—to grab the best from both of you. Anthony, mentioned earlier, is a former musician and likened his friendship with Errol as a kind of harmony, an arrangement of *different* notes that come together to create something that cannot be achieved by one note. "One note would be unison, not harmony," he said.

Another creative pair, composer John Williams and filmmaker Steven Spielberg, have been collaborating on Oscar-winning films like *E.T.* and *Saving Private Ryan* for more than four decades. In a 2014 interview, they appear very at ease with each other, and their conversation flows as they describe working together.[8]

Williams appears the more introverted of the two; he speaks in measured tones, while the extroverted Spielberg takes up more airtime to make his points. They each point to the ease of collaboration as time goes on. "As I get better, I know how to use him better," Spielberg explains. As is true for Errol and Anthony, John Williams describes the dynamic of fun in their partnership. He can tell by Spielberg's eyes and facial expression whether he "has it" or not. "Even when I don't have it, we are having fun anyway."

Instead of getting irritated, partners in all fields learn to read each other's nonverbal signals over time just like Spielberg and Williams do. These cues become gateways to gain deeper understanding of the alien's point of view, allowing him or her to move back and forth with relative ease.

⚠ How Accepting the Alien Can Break Down

Not Realizing That Your Strengths Are My Weaknesses

Not stopping to consider differences in personality can cause problems. My younger daughter, Jessie Kahnweiler, is an LA-based filmmaker who has had the opportunity to work with many introverted pros on her film crews. On a complex video shoot she hired Liam, an experienced and highly regarded introverted director of photography. As they were scoping out the shots, extroverted Jessie spilled over with ideas and could barely contain her enthusiasm. She sensed that Liam was not sharing the excitement she had hoped he would. Jessie would text him ideas for locations, and he would respond with short, terse replies.

On the day of the shoot, Liam appeared with a large notebook of carefully thought-out shots that incorporated many of the ideas she had been pitching him. Jessie realized that Liam was listening and engaging with her all along; just quietly and in his space. He actually had a deep love and understanding of the project but was approaching it in his internally focused, methodical way. "Liam's strengths were my weaknesses," Jessie shared. "He is a planner and needed time to sort things out in his head. That is exactly what was needed. I think introverts have a confidence because they trust their minds so much. They spend a great deal of time alone thinking about things and processing. He is not going to change and neither am I. God knows, we only need one of me!"

It happens; even the most accepting partners lose their patience at times. The culprit behind it? Usually stress.

Stress can be a good thing; it can energize us and get us moving. However, we can react in ways that are not productive for the partnership or ultimately ourselves. Here are a few ways stress undermines accepting the alien in an introvert/extrovert pair.

Introverts Shut Down, Extroverts Talk More

When stress happens, we often go into overdrive on our personality characteristics. Introverts shut down and extroverts talk more. This creates tension as the introvert is thinking, *Won't she ever shut up?* and the extrovert is thinking, *What is going on in her head?!*

Errol and Anthony, the Australian partners, had one of their few big disagreements over a request from Errol to add a color to a design that Anthony and his team had been working on for a while. Introverted Anthony responded by shutting down and actually not speaking to Errol for a day. "I was pretty riled by it all. Nothing else was said for the rest of the workday." They clarified that what Errol had meant was that he wanted to see the color in the design, not that it actually had to change. They restarted their communication and all was good again. When opposites don't do that, however, these misfires keep happening, leading to potentially irreparable explosions.

Outside Stress Can Also Take a Toll

The 2008 recession was a turning point for Han, an introverted Korean consultant, and his extroverted Chinese partner, Mei. They co-owned a risk management/consulting firm and had been doing very well as a partnership and company until the recession.

"Mei was a natural saleswoman, but unfortunately made promises that we couldn't deliver on. Her enthusiasm and strong client relationships were assets and overrode my concerns. That is, until the consulting gigs started dropping. We were not delivering on our promises, and our service started to slip. This was unacceptable to me. Mei was not interested in scaling back the business, and we parted ways. It was definitely the stress of the recession that made the difference. I think we would still be together if our values had not been tested in that way."

Han had just purchased a new house and had mortgage payments on his mind. Mei was the sole breadwinner for her family and also felt a lot riding on her shoulders. These economic pressures had a significant impact on the duo. In other cases, problems with children, spouses, parents, and friends are all factors that can significantly complicate the communication flow between opposites.

These outside stressful events like a department move or a change in managers can bring out our fears and lower our tolerance levels. Introverts become more internally focused. Extroverts go into high-energy mode. Clashes occur more frequently. And these moments also provide the true test of whether a partnership will survive.

Several years ago, my twenty-something daughter, Lindsey, an extrovert, was describing her relationship with her introverted boyfriend, Adam, now her husband. "Mom," she said, "we never have had a fight." I smiled and (uncharacteristically) didn't say much except, "Really?"

Then they moved into a small apartment in Washington, DC. I gave her a call the first week to check in. "Guess what, Mom, we have had several arguments this week! And over little things like where to put the couch!" There is nothing like the outside stress of a move or close living quarters to bring out our irritations and lower our tolerance levels.

Solutions: Keep Focused on Results

There are several steps you can take to keep your eye on the outcomes you want to achieve together and the genius in your partnership.

Learn About Personality Styles

Learn about your own style and your partner's. Take a personality instrument or an interpersonal skills class so that you can learn what you bring to the partnership. Keep aware of when problems are your issues and not your partner's. The breakthrough comes when you learn that your partner is not intending to make you crazy, but is just wired differently. With that knowledge comes great relief, and best of all, much less judgment.

Table 3.1 Introvert/Extrovert Differences

Introverts	Extroverts
Energize in quiet time	Energize with other people
Think about their ideas	Talk out their ideas
Focus on depth	Focus on breadth
Get to know someone and then share private info	Readily share private information
Thrive in one-on-one conversations	Get energy from larger groups

Learn to Speak Their Language

You can build on that self-awareness. Knowing that your introvert craves time to think quietly, or that your extrovert is dying to think aloud, is an important clue for flexing or adjusting your behavior. You will find that taking a walk on the other side will help your own growth.

One of the first members of introverted Amazon CEO Jeff Bezos's team, Jeff Holden, was known as a "fast talker." In Brad Stone's book *The Everything Store*, Stone writes, "[Holden] spoke so rapidly that Bezos liked to joke that Holden 'taught me to listen faster.' "[9] Holden had a personal relationship with Bezos and was a "versatile innovator" who contributed greatly to the growth of Amazon. His impact went beyond business results to positively influence CEO Bezos's communication skills.

Just as Holden impacted Bezos's listening acumen, you will find yourself being influenced by the opposites around you. You may find yourself having experiences like those of introverted business partner Arlene, who forced herself to attend a professional meeting and actually learned to come out of her shell, or of Tamika the extrovert who said, "I am an E working on being quiet. I shut up in meetings, and when I speak I really have something to say!"

Over time, if extroverts can take the time to let introverts reveal themselves, introverts open up. And if introverts are patient with the ongoing outpourings of extroverts, they may find themselves catching some of that ebullience.

Accept that You Can't Change Them

The Serenity Prayer applies here: "Grant me the serenity to accept the things I cannot change, the courage to change the things I can, and the wisdom to know the difference." You will never change another person, nor should you. Yet the stubborn nature of two strong-willed people can cause one to wish the other would think faster or talk less. Ironically, the more you lay off trying to change them, the less it will bother you. Once you let go of this false hope of molding them to your desired image, everyone can relax and life gets a lot easier.

This quote by David Kiersey from his book, *Please Understand Me*, makes the point another way:

> *If I do not want what you want, please try not to tell me that my want is wrong.*
>
> *Or if I believe other than you, at least pause before you correct my view.*
>
> *Or if my emotion is less than yours, or more, given the same circumstances, try not to ask me to feel more strongly or weakly.*
>
> *Or yet if I act, or fail to act, in the manner of your design for action, let me be.*
>
> *I do not, for the moment at least, ask you to understand me. That will come only when you are willing to give up changing me into a copy of you.*[10]

Remove the Elephant from the Room

Talking about your differences gives them legitimacy. This is particularly important in the beginning of your work together, but holds true throughout the relationship.

One new team member in a Singaporean import company found herself in a sea of extroverts. She made a preemptive move with her extroverted teammate by explaining that when her door was closed, it meant she needed quiet time. It did not mean that she was angry or frustrated with them. Knowing this took away the mystery of the closed door and allowed the extroverts to relax.

Work on Adapting One Small Thing at a Time

As an extrovert, see how it works when you decide to dim the lights to reduce the external stimulation. Or what happens when, as an introvert, you intentionally practice eye contact for a few minutes longer than usual in order to connect with your opposite. Observe the reaction in your partner. You may be surprised at the positive impact even this small move can make.

In addition to connecting more effectively with your opposite, you will find that this deliberate stretching develops a previously untapped side of yourself. You will have a richer array of tools to draw from when dealing with your current opposite and future partners.

Create a Shorthand for Communicating

Create a code, a way to stop the action when you are off course. Extrovert Mark House and introvert Maureen Blackwell teach at universities and consult together. They will turn to each other in person or on the phone and say, "We are missing each other" whenever their dialogue is breaking down.

They also have a helpful phrase that Mark started using and now Maureen has adopted. When they are talking and one of them goes off topic, one will say, "Let me go on a tangent," signaling the conversational sidebar. It allows the listener to follow the flow of the speaker's words more easily. The listener can go with the flow and not worry about following ideas that aren't fully formed. Initiated by the more extemporaneous talker partner Mark, they both find it amusing that now Maureen is using it as a tool in their free-flowing dialogues.

Give It Time

Introvert/extrovert opposite partners often have tremendous appreciation for what their opposite brings to the work relationship, and that respect has grown over time.

As you will see in Chapter 6, "Destroy the Dislike," one pair of consultants, Billie Alban and Barbara Bunker, have become dear friends. They travel all over the world together and have learned to appreciate their individual qualities over more than three decades. Barbara, the introvert, recently realized that she hadn't brought a book on the plane with her in years because in earlier days Billie would talk her ear off throughout the flight while she was trying to read. There was an affectionate and accepting tone in her voice as she described this scene.

Meet Regularly and Talk

Successful introvert/extrovert partners give each other updates and honest feedback regularly about how things are going. They address problems quickly and don't let them fester. One introverted CEO rarely comes into the office, but his extroverted second-in-command knows he can always reach him late at night on email to get a quick response. They also have quick chats whenever needed, and to the rest of staff these two appear to be in synch. Figuring out what methods work for both of them is key, and they revisit that key from time to time.

Summary: Respect the Wiring

Because extroverts and introverts are wired so differently, working together gives these opposites many chances to disagree or even reject each other. Yet learning to accept the alien in each other opens up more than a significantly enriched relationship: more creative opportunities present themselves to the pair who does the hard work of acceptance. Disciplining yourself to learn how and why your opposite sees the world differently is work, but the work carries rewards that far outweigh your investment. You will feel almost as if you've learned to speak another language, and in relationship terms, you will have done just that.

Questions to Consider

1. In what situations can you watch for your opposite's nonverbal signals?

2. How will you remember to take a deep breath the next time you are losing patience with your opposite?

3. What can you do to take a time-out when you are facing a stressful situation?

4. What shorthand signal or phrase can you develop with your opposite when you are "missing each other"?

5. Have you accepted that you cannot change your opposite? How will this belief help you in working with them?

Chapter 4

Bring on the Battles

"We often hate each other, but it's the kind of hatred that's like flint and steel—the sparks that come out make it worth the while."[11]

—Penn Jillette on his long-time partner in magic, Teller

Bring on the Battles—see disagreement as necessary to arrive at better outcomes because you challenge each other to come up with better solutions together than you would alone.

Back in 1956, Dr. Alice Mary Stewart, a physician and epidemiologist, came out with a shocking article published by the British medical journal *The Lancet*. Her article cited data showing that the X-rays taken of pregnant mothers actually caused childhood cancer. Sadly, the medical establishment did not immediately act upon her findings. Instead, it took twenty-five years for doctors to stop X-raying pregnant women.

Through those years, she worked closely with George Kneale, a statistician who was instrumental to her success. He helped her to fuel her determination and persistence, leading to the eventual ending of a tragically harmful medical practice.

In her TED Talk, Dare to Disagree,[12] management thinker Margaret Heffernan said, "So for twenty-five years, Alice Stewart had a very big fight on her hands. So how did she know that she was right? George Kneale was pretty much everything that Alice wasn't. Alice was very outgoing and sociable, and George was a recluse. Alice was very warm and empathetic with her patients. George frankly preferred numbers to people. But he said this fantastic thing about their working relationship: "My job is to prove Dr. Stewart wrong." He actively sought disconfirmation. He used different ways of looking at her models, at her statistics, different ways of crunching the data in order to disprove her. He saw his job as creating conflict around her theories. By creating pushback,

George sharpened her thinking and made her theory more convincing.

Successful opposites use their differences to challenge each other's conventional thinking and blast apart their assumptions. Like opposites Alice and George, they bring on the battles, and the world benefits from the results of their genius.

Why Bringing on the Battles Matters

It's Best for the Organization

Introverts and extroverts who work well together are fortunate. They can pull out the best thinking from each other, like blending two brains into one. They push toward each other, pull away from each other, and eventually reach a resolution that incorporates different views. Extrovert Betsy Polk and introvert Maggie Ellis Chotas are authors of *Power Through Partnership: How Women Lead Better Together*. They write about the value of dealing with their conflicts head-on. "We've come to realize that even in the toughest tug of wars we want what is best for Mulberry [their firm] and each other."[13]

You Reach a Better Solution

Successful opposites learn to dance with each other by playing to each preference when facing potential conflict. Introverted Ricardo and his extroverted business partner Jose described a recent conflict about whether to add an assessment tool to their online business's offerings. They had run the idea for the service by their prime client, who expressed interest in learning more.

Jose had a lot of ideas about how this tool could work and was energized by the possibilities. All he wanted to do was talk about it. Ricardo, typically the more cautious of the two, wasn't sure they could deliver the service with the stated customer requirements. Both men could feel the temperature rising as they gave voice to their differing views.

They each approached the next steps using their strengths. Jose knew that more talk would overwhelm Ricardo, who was mulling over the plan, so he grabbed another colleague, a "talking partner," to give voice to his ideas and pop out solutions. Ricardo, on the other hand, went to his work area alone for a few days and mapped out the process, including a timetable and potential risks. Though Jose was ready to pull the trigger and Ricardo needed more time, they avoided a blow-up and emerged with a terrific solution. The client signed off on the new service. By bringing on the battle in a way that catered to their opposite styles, this team drew a clear win.

Disagreements Can Be Paths to Your Outcome

Successful opposites accept that decisions come with conflict and that conflict is normal, natural, and necessary.

They know that disagreements open the path to an outcome. When you walk through business problems together, it isn't a linear process. You may get stuck on one disagreement for a while before you can move on. Successful opposites get that.

Even long-time best work buddies like Ricky Woolverton, an extroverted inside sales manager, and Liz Braden, an introverted training director, have disagreements. Back when they started working together, the company president matched them up hoping to balance out their personalities. And it worked until one time. "I was supervising Ricky, and I was forced to run a tight ship. He thought it was okay to take a salesman to the airport when he was supposed to be on the phones and decided to ignore my direction." As an extrovert, Ricky took action without mulling it over, and as an introvert Liz kept her feelings inside. "We were mad at each other for a week."

Talking about the situation after it occurred allowed them both to move on and be more productive. Their communication has vastly improved since then. Liz has learned from Ricky and through interpersonal skills training to see the necessity of conflict. She is less afraid of it. "Now, I take that extra minute and ask myself, 'Where is that person coming from?'" she said.

Extroverted Ricky agreed to speak in lower tones and actually listen to what Liz is requesting of him.

It continues to work well as a way to manage their disagreements.

⚠ How Bringing on the Battles Breaks Down

Seeing One Partner as More Important

Former auto executive Robert Lutz described his work with opposite Robert Eaton, CEO of Chrysler from 1993 to 1998, in the language of an extrovert describing an introvert. Lutz wrote, "A gentle leader of modest charisma and command presence . . . Bob [Eaton] was experienced, polite, well-spoken, and knew the business. He showed the mature, calm confidence and self-assured manner that had been honed in decades of facing upward and looking good at GM. We (Lutz and Eaton) had a good sharing of responsibilities."[14] Together they made a great deal of money for the company.

The next chapter in Chrysler's history was very different. Benz-Daimler and Chrysler combined the firms in 1998, and a new CEO, Jurgen Schrempp, came on board. Lutz wrote that Schrempp "was a tall man with a powerful, commanding physique and a stentorian voice . . . a brash giant." It was apparent that this new leader saw himself as more important.

"It was pretty clear that this was not going to be a jointly run company." Lutz watched these opposites have problems from the start, ending with Eaton's departure. In summing up that unfortunate chapter, Lutz said that

Eaton "ran a great company . . . and created enormous wealth for Chrysler's shareholders," but "Bob Eaton had his reputation unfairly tarnished."

Extrovert Lutz valued introvert Eaton's quiet contributions and the opposites thrived, but Eaton's next partner either couldn't or wouldn't see his introverted partner as an equal.

Hiding Your Concerns

Kendra is an introverted lawyer and was a new mom working on a big case. Her extroverted business partner Carolyn's patience was being tested. Kendra's breastfeeding breaks, hormone rollercoaster rides, and leaving work early to arrive at the daycare center before closing were becoming the norm. Carolyn often found herself picking up the pieces from Kendra's tasks and clocking up to two additional late nights a week.

Carolyn expressed frustration about the clients' increasing demands and started taking out her anger on other people in the firm. Kendra knew she was not pulling her weight and felt stressed and guilty about her role in the situation. As an introvert, she internalized her concerns and kept them buried. The problem was that neither of them brought up the elephant in the room—the workload imbalance. After they blew an important client deadline, Carolyn and Kendra met one evening over a glass of wine and ended up talking for four hours, honestly airing their emotions and concerns. They brainstormed solutions to the workload issues and eventually came up with an agreement they both could live with.

Acknowledging that their goal was to meet their clients' needs, they put together a strong case to the senior partner for temporary help. This solution made all the difference and repaired their strained relationship.

Under stress, we often act out in ways that are not helpful to resolving conflict. As an introvert, Kendra internalized her feelings and did not bring up the issues between them, while Carolyn acted out passive aggressively. Neither approach helped resolve the conflicts, even when they both wanted to reach the same outcome—to serve the client in the best way possible.

Losing Sight of Your Shared Vision

One introvert/extrovert married couple I interviewed, Achir, an introverted woman and Ishar, an extroverted man, are business owners originally from India. They built a printing business together in Washington, DC. They are moderately profitable and always incorporating new technology into the business. They each began working together with the hope of building a better life and providing for their family. Although they are proud of what they have accomplished, they have been through a lot to get there.

Individually, they each told me about some of the stressors that took them away from their vision of creating a strong family business; one that adapted to the changing printing industry. The pressure to keep up with technology was a major stressor.

Achir described disagreements between them about new purchases for the business. Ishar admitted that he sometimes plunged ahead without consulting his spouse on what he considered necessary investments. As an introvert and influenced by her cultural influences (for example, don't bring up conflict), Achir kept her feelings inside and said, "I don't want to dwell on our disagreements too much." But the problem was her feelings would pile up.

These mutual hurts and misunderstandings moved them further from their shared vision of creating a dynamic business that could support their family. It would have helped them to bring the battle to each other. One can't help wonder how directly dealing with their frustrations and conflicts might have opened up even greater possibilities for strategic growth and personal satisfaction from their business.

Solutions: To Help You Bring on the Battle

Remember Energy Differences

Accept that your partner's introverted energy may wane from too much people time working on conflict resolution, or your extroverted colleague's buzz might get her too hyped up when conflict emerges. Remember that introverts need to carefully consider ideas in their head before speaking, and extroverts are ready to *get moving* already. Also consider that your introvert will need breaks and your extrovert will deflate with too much downtime.

Tell 'Em What You Need

You can set the foundation for clear communication when you bring on the battles. Let your partner know specifically what you need.

Self-described "raging extrovert" Lisa McLeod is a sales leadership consultant and author. She and her introverted business partner and husband, Bob McLeod, avoid flare-ups by stating what they require in the moment. As Lisa puts it, "I am a verbal processor and I need to talk. I depend on Bob for my energy." She understands that when she is calling from out of town and he doesn't answer he is in his introverted space. And when she does connect with Bob, Lisa is very clear about saying, "I need a half-hour to talk about it. Is now a good time?" If it is not, he'll say, "Not now," instead of "No." She says, "I know it is not a personal rejection, and we will reconvene when he is better able to focus."

Manage Crises Together

When the inevitable crises occur, put your heads together and figure out a way through. That often means drawing on the partner in the pair who is better suited to meet the problem at hand.

Table 4.1 Helpful Questions for Bringing on the Battle

When to Ask	What to Ask
Before a conflict	▪ What is it I really want? ▪ Do I understand what my partner really wants? ▪ How invested am I in the outcome? How invested is my partner?
During a conflict	▪ Do I allow my introverted partner to communicate with me in writing and one-on-one conversations? ▪ Do I allow my extroverted partner to communicate with me through talking things out? ▪ Am I letting my emotions hijack my rational thinking? Am I letting my rational thinking hijack my emotions? ▪ Are we taking time-outs during our discussion of the problem? ▪ Does it make sense to bring in an outside person to help us resolve the disagreement? Who might that be? ▪ Does it make sense to agree on a trial solution first? ▪ Have we set a date to implement the solution? ▪ When will we meet again?
After a conflict	▪ How is the solution working? ▪ What should we tweak? ▪ What have we learned from this experience? ▪ What should we do differently the next time a conflict arises?

Anthony, the co-founder of the Australian online training company, said that one time they were stuck in the "stuff" of the problem and not dealing with a client problem at a higher relationship level. This was clearly his extroverted partner Errol's turf. Errol picked up the phone and arranged to see the client immediately. By taking full responsibility for where things had gone wrong, Errol defused the situation and got the relationship back on track. The client went from being one of the pair's most troublesome, stressful clients to being one of their most loyal.

Bring in a Third Party to Break Through an Impasse

When my introverted spouse, Bill, and I were writing our first book together, we reached one of several impasses: managing the timeline. In typical fashion, Bill was way ahead of me on his section of the manuscript. After several unproductive conversations, we decided to call our editor in Cambridge, England. I can hear Ailsa's calming voice now as she gently suggested to Bill that he relax and I "get moving." Turning to an objective outsider helped us break the tension and start communicating more civilly again. We finished on time, though not without a few more impasses and calls to England. Turning to Ailsa was a strategic move for us. It took a third party to help us get unstuck and see a way forward.

Take a Time-Out

Michael, an extroverted salesperson, was getting little visible reaction from his sales team partner, Derrick. He kicked it into high gear to try even harder to convince Derrick why they needed to purchase more product to sell. Unfortunately, Michael's "passionate entreaties" had the opposite effect, and Derrick walked away from the discussion.

When Michael dialed down his behavior by taking a breath and listening to Derrick's concerns, he could address them one by one, and the partners had a rational problem-solving session.

You may be together a great deal in the beginning of your partnership or at critical points throughout. But too much time together means you can get lost in the duo and lose your sense of self as well as your unique point of view.

You can also definitely get tired of each other. Ask any retired couple who find themselves together all day! Sometimes taking a time-out is the best workaround to help you regroup and reconvene, ready to engage with a clear head and heart.

As mentioned in the chapter on Accepting the Alien, during conflict and stress we exaggerate our strengths. For instance, it is natural to talk more often and louder as an extrovert or retreat into yourself as an introvert. Resist the tendency to amplify your natural traits. Take a few moments to stop and think. Even a few minutes of quiet

will help you consider your next step. And, by the way . . .
it may be to do nothing!

Walk and Talk

Consider moving your conversation outside the doors of
your office. This strategy serves the needs of both extroverts and introverts. Why? Extroverts think aloud, and
talking out their ideas while walking around helps them
gain clarity about their positions. They can also ask questions of their partners without seeming like a prosecuting
attorney with the introvert on the witness stand. Introverts will respond to the relaxed pace. They also will con-
serve energy by not having to concentrate on making eye
contact and other in-your-face listening behaviors.

When you let the juices flow by getting up and
moving, new ideas spring up and you will see solutions
together. Thought leader and a proponent of these walking meetings, Nilofer Merchant, writes, "After a few
hundred of these meetings, I've started noticing some
unanticipated side benefits. . . . I can actually listen better when I am walking next to someone than when I'm
across from them in some coffee shop. There's something
about being side-by-side that puts the problem or ideas
before us, and us working on it together."[15]

Summary: Bringing on the Battles Can Preempt a War

In the hands of committed opposites, bringing on the battles can lead to original solutions and breakthroughs that benefit opposites and their clients. Conflict-facing skills include honoring what energizes each partner, talking about what each of you needs, dealing with crises together, and turning to a third party when necessary. It also means taking a time-out, and even talking about the conflict while walking beside each other rather than when facing each other. The more high stakes the situation, the more important it is for opposites to bring on the battles as an outcome-focused team.

Questions to Consider

1. How do you take opportunities to challenge your opposite's thinking?

2. In what ways do you use your individual strengths to handle crises?

3. Do you consider your partner's introvert or extrovert preferences when approaching him or her with sensitive information?

4. What are the ways in which you carve out regular talk time?

5. When can you bring in a third party to resolve conflict?

Chapter 5

Cast the Character

"If I irritated him by a certain methodical slowness in my mentality, that irritation served only to make his own flame-like intuitions and impressions flash up more vividly and swiftly. Such was my humble role in our alliance."

—Watson, speaking of Sherlock Holmes[16]

Cast the Character: Know each person's role in a scenario and cast them so that you bring out your opposite's best. Opposites share the credit no matter what role they take.

One of the largest Internet companies in the world, Alibaba, has been called the equivalent of PayPal, Amazon, and eBay all rolled into one. Its founder and former CEO, Jack Ma, is the heart and soul of the company. It hasn't been unusual for this extrovert to dress up in costume and sing songs from *The Lion King* to Alibaba's more than sixteen thousand employees.

In 2013, Ma turned the CEO's reins over to his trusted partner, Jonathon Lu, who is described as Ma's "corporate alter-ego." Lu is used to operating behind the scenes. Lu said, "We complement each other very well. He looks forward and outside of the box; I focus on the present."[17]

When Lu was managing the South China sales region for Alibaba.com, he drove Ma around to meet customers across Guangdong. On these rides, Lu offered his ideas about how to fine-tune sales incentives. "It was a time for us to really get to know each other—him talking and me listening, him sleeping and me driving." And with the characteristic good humor of genius opposites, Lu said, "Ninety percent of the time, it is him talking. Then I say yes."

Though he has stepped down, Ma is still very much involved as the executive chair and public face of Alibaba, in addition to being the richest man in China. Ma made the handoff to Lu because he knew that Lu could lead the company forward, building on his unique strengths.

Let's look at why genius opposites like these two succeed when they cast the right character.

Why Casting the Characters Matters

Opposites Can Step Into Their Strengths

Magic happens when opposites tap into their strengths to play their natural roles. For instance, many opposites will use this style difference to their advantage by leveraging the easy-flowing conversation of the extrovert with certain customers, and not thrusting introverts into those awkward situations.

This is true for twenty-five-year veteran partners introverted Shyam and extroverted Veer, who gravitate to their natural strengths. Shyam, chief technology officer of an information technology company, easily interacts with his long-time government clients, but when it comes to meeting new people, he is much less at ease. He turns over the meet-and-greet interactions to Veer, the CEO, who thrives in these extroverted scenarios. By tag-teaming the sales responsibilities in this way, they are able to continue to drive revenues for their firm.

Conversely, sometimes casting the right character means trying on your opposite's strengths in order to get the job done. Author of *Give and Take*, Adam Grant researched the success factors of salespeople and found that many of them exhibited what he called "ambivert" traits; they exhibited both introvert and extrovert traits. Grant believes that organizations benefit "from training highly extroverted salespeople to model some of the quiet, reserved tendencies of their more introverted peers."[18] Extending their ranges does not diminish either the introvert's or the extrovert's natural strengths, but it can serve their shared purpose extremely well.

Having a Straight Man/Woman Works for Opposites

Many opposites build on introvert and extrovert differences by casting the introvert as the "straight man." The "out-there" person is the extrovert. Author Joshua Wolf Shenk calls these straight men "offstage partners." The charismatic Martin Luther King Jr., described the lower-key Ralph Abernathy Jr., as his "sidekick and warm up."[19] Abernathy would warm up the crowd, give the crowd the facts on the ground, and rouse them to fight. Dr. King would follow him and then give his sermon.

The late comic George Burns and his wife, Gracie Allen, were another perfect example of this dynamic. She acted the "out-there," ditzy wife, and he was the calm husband. In describing them, author Roger Rosenblatt wrote, "The essence of the straight man is that he gives. He gives the best lines, the stage and the spotlight. By giving, he creates the show. . . ."[20] They appeared together because the mutually complementary roles linked them. Their outcome depended on each one playing a set role.[21]

The Right Casting Leads to
Unexpected Positive Outcomes

Playing your natural role may lead to positive results that you didn't intend. Twenty-something introvert Charlotte Ashlock, digital producer and editor at publishing company Berrett-Koehler, reflects on a high school experience with her friend Betsy that illustrates this well.

"Betsy and I were both members of our school's Destination Imagination team, a club that did competitive improvisation and problem solving. During team meetings, I wanted to be very focused on practicing and preparing for the upcoming competition. Betsy was more willing to spend the time relaxing and socializing during meetings. I sometimes thought, *Why doesn't anyone else care about working?* and felt frustrated. My fears were realized when our team arrived at the competition less prepared than I wanted us to be.

"Minutes before going on stage, all of us were full of panic. Then Betsy grabbed one of our props, a fake head of lettuce, and announced in a grand, triumphant, and vaguely silly manner, 'So long as we have the lettuce, we cannot fail!' We burst out laughing, shouted, 'THE LETTUCE!' and went onto the stage prepared to have fun. Our team didn't win (in fact, we were in the bottom 20 percent), but I had an unbelievable amount of fun and felt very bonded with my teammates. I also realized that

Betsy's values of laughter and team spirit were just as important as my values of hard work and seriousness."

In Charlotte's story, the positive impact on the team outweighed any frustrations she might have felt. By letting Betsy be Betsy, the team connected and went on to win several regional championships.

⚠ How Casting the Character Breaks Down

Roles Are Unclear or Unfair

A humorous example of this can be seen in a particular *I Love Lucy* episode, a 1950s comedy television show in which two starring couples, the Ricardos and the Mertzes, decide to buy a diner together. They decide that "one couple has the know-how and one has the name."[22] Unfortunately, this results in Fred and Ethel, the couple with the know-how, doing all the work! They are in the back cooking hamburgers while Lucy and Ricky Ricardo are meeting and greeting patrons. Feeling resentful, Fred and Ethel walk out, leaving Ricky and Lucy to handle everything. That doesn't work, obviously.

As the episode unravels, they even end up splitting the restaurant in half, fighting for the one inebriated customer who wanders into the restaurant. None of the solutions they try is effective.

Perhaps this episode is a bit of an exaggeration, but not clarifying who does what can lead to other problems as well. Stephanie, the introverted video producer you will meet later, described a disconnect with her partner, Jane, in this way: "At first Jane and I were both doing each stage of the process: call the inquiry, write the quote, and follow up. With both of us doing each stage of the sales process, it was very difficult to know the whole picture. We lost track of who followed up with whom and when. . . ." It caused them to lose business and potential income.

One Person Takes All the Credit

Daryl Hall and John Oates (called Hall and Oates) are well-known musicians who have played together for more than forty-five years. They have never had a public rift. John is seen as the introverted sideman to the extroverted Daryl Hall, even though he plays a pivotal role in the duo's success.

When asked how he feels about being seen as the sideman, the introverted Oates said, "I am okay with it because I don't think of myself that way. Other people may, the world may, but that's fine. I kind of look at it in a more Zen way. you can't have a beautiful sunset without a horizon. Daryl (Hall) is a very in-your-face person when it comes to performing, and he has a tremendous voice. The fact that his voice became the signature sound of Hall and Oates is just the way it is."[23]

Unfortunately, not all opposites are so gracious and accepting of such contrasting roles. Author Adam Grant describes the devastating impact of taking all the credit in telling the story of polio vaccine researcher Jonas Salk. After the vaccine had been successfully disseminated, "a press conference was held where Salk gave no credit to the six researchers in his lab who were major contributors to his efforts to develop the vaccine. His moment of taking sole credit haunted him for the rest of his career," wrote Grant. "His colleagues rejected him, he never won a Nobel Prize, and he was never elected to the prestigious National Academy of Sciences. People really held it against him that he had grandstanded like that and done the most uncollegial thing that you could imagine."[24] In this case the consequences were damaging to both the team and to Salk himself.

Trap the Other in Rigid Expectations

Rashid, an introverted architect, works with Sari, an extroverted designer. He has become used to her stopping by to describe her latest project idea. They often have a good laugh together. In fact, he gets a kick out of her chatty drop-ins. He actually welcomes these breaks in his routine.

One day, however, he was particularly engrossed in a complex problem and was bent over his desk, headphones on. Sari flew in, describing her latest passion, and Rashid looked up with a definitive scowl. After talking for another minute, she picked up on his mood and angrily marched away. It took a few days for the ice to thaw.

Like Sari expecting Rashid never to deviate from being an attentive, friendly listener, we expect our partners to always behave as we are used to them behaving. Because they are human, there are times when they will deviate from type.

We can let customers pigeonhole us by seeking out one partner over the other, even when either is perfectly capable of handling a situation. Adelaide Lancaster and Amy Abrams are co-owners of a NYC-based company. Adelaide is introverted and Amy is extroverted. Adelaide remarked, "People typecast us a lot. I would imagine it is a similar challenge to that experienced by siblings and twins. I become known as the detail/data one and Amy as the social/friendly one."[25] One person's greater strength is not necessarily something that the other person completely lacks.

Solutions: You Can Cast Characters and Still Be Flexible

Get Your Own House in Order First

Your differences as extroverts and introverts are great enough that it makes sense to gain your own sense of self and what you have to offer before embarking on a relationship with your opposite. Famous ice cream entrepreneurs Burton Baskin and Irvine Robbins began their joint business after they each had run successful businesses of their own. Only after they had individual success did their partnership work.[26]

You may need to enhance and fine-tune your skill set and get some experience before embarking on a joint venture in your business or organization. That way you enter the relationship knowing what role you can play best and what contributions you are looking for from your opposite.

Be an Advocate for Your Opposite

Extroverted Brook, vice president and branch manager at a financial institution, says that she constantly "throws her employee Monica curve balls, but she keeps the steady pace and doesn't miss a beat!" The outspoken Brook sees part of her role as speaking up to senior management about the strong results Monica achieves. Though Brook would like Monica to be more visible and sing her own praises, she draws on her own strength as a talker and promoter to play the advocate role. As an extrovert, you can use your tendency to be assertive to speak up for others who are more reticent to "brag on themselves."

Introverts can advocate for their opposites as well. Jose, an introverted VP of operations with a calm temperament, played "damage control" at a customer presentation. Several extroverted sales team members were very expressive and shared their strong enthusiasm about the rollout of a new product. Nicole, the customer, had several questions about how the product would be integrated into her company's existing process and was very skeptical of the "rah rah attitude" she was hearing from yet another sales team. She was concerned that it was all talk and that there would be little follow-up action.

Recognizing Nicole's concern, Jose performed damage control. He met with her privately, conducted a quiet, focused conversation, and patiently addressed all of Nicole's questions. By balancing the extroverts' hyper-enthusiasm with his calm reassurance, he restored the team's credibility with the customer and ultimately made the sale.

As an introvert, you can use your strengths in listening, observation, and calm, reasoned conversation to temper reactions and avoid misunderstandings, especially when extroverts react in the moment.

Break Out of Your Expected Role Occasionally

When you step out of character, or use traits that aren't as comfortable, you stretch and grow. Your "opposite muscle" will inevitably get stronger.

Jonathon Lu, the former Alibaba CEO, committed to adapting to his role, even though he knew it would require extroverted behavior. After taking over the company, he said, "Our plan is that Jack Ma (the former CEO) doesn't need to come out so often," Lu said. "I will face the public more often, but this needs time and I also need to improve myself."

By stretching into more extroverted behavior at meetings so that she talked with many people, introverted Arlene Cohn stopped clinging to her husband and business partner, Steve. She realized as she did this that she was making friends and contacts in their line of business, increasing her value to the partnership.

Look at what introverted or extroverted tendencies you can stretch into and try them on. This "cross-training" will allow two positive outcomes: your opposite and others will learn to rely on you for a wider range of support, and you will gain confidence in your own abilities as you each expand your individual roles.

Match Tasks to Your Type

In their complex and often intense change management projects, consultants Emily and Dick Axelrod find it an advantage to match their client assignments by personality. They ask, "Which of us will the client be more comfortable with?" and that person takes the lead. This is a fluid discussion and often relies on their understanding of introvert and extrovert strengths.

"I create a calmer and safer presence," says the introverted Dick, "but if we need to organize people quickly or we need more energy, Emily steps in. When we deliver feedback, she might give the feedback while I make sure that people understand it and are dealing with it well," he explains.

The Axelrods' clients often comment that this duality offers them tremendous value before, during, and after the projects. Their clients get much more "bang for their buck" than if just one of the pair were involved.

Own your strengths and use them with your opposite to get things done. Think about the roles you take in terms of what you each have to offer your client, and then adjust your client-facing behavior accordingly.

Get It in Writing

Successful business partners agree that they need to be clear about the terms of their agreement, and they often put that in writing. Michael, one of my introverted business colleagues, writes me extensive emails with the proposed details of our different responsibilities. I understand that he is using his strengths of preparation and writing. We then schedule time to talk things out, my extroverted preference. By playing to both of our preferences, his writing and my talking, we clarify each of our roles and solidify our plans.

Provide On-the-Spot Coaching

Coaching, including giving and receiving feedback to your partner, is a vital way to nurture a team of opposites. Introverted Asia, a senior vice president of audit, has open communication with her chief financial officer, Lauren, who is an extrovert. When Lauren is overwhelming

Table 5.1 On-the-Spot Coaching Tips

Giving Feedback	Getting Feedback
Ask "Is this a good time for feedback?"	Say whether this time works for you
Be clear and specific about what you observed and what you are asking for	Ask for a specific example of what your partner observed if you need more information
Ask open-ended questions: "How do you see it?" "Have you thought about this?"	Paraphrase to make sure you understand
Be specific about what you would like to see happen next time the situation occurs	Acknowledge the feedback and consider a possible change
Say thank you	Say thank you

the team with her rapid-fire diatribe, Asia reminds her to breathe. This on-the-spot coaching slows Lauren down, helping her to get her message across with more impact. In fact, Lauren has even started asking Asia for additional feedback on other aspects of her management style.

As an extrovert, you can support your introverted partner's stepping into more visible roles, such as meetings. Vijay, a confident and extroverted venture capitalist, was instrumental in helping his friend Ben prepare for their pitch to investors. He had Ben rehearse aloud several times until Ben felt at ease with his presentation. Vijay knew how to help Ben by playing to his preference for preparation. As a result, Ben did a terrific job of making his points and getting buy-in to his new business idea.

Summary: Here's Where Outcomes Can Improve Exponentially

When opposites work together, they can step fully into their strengths for the benefit of the project in ways that teams without opposites could not. Mutually complementary roles often emerge when opposites team up to meet an objective, and the outcome can be better than anyone anticipated. That happens only when the roles are clear and partners share the credit, refusing to allow simple typecasting to blur the work they've done to stretch toward each other.

The highest-functioning opposites advocate for each other, break out of strict role definitions, and agree to accept coaching from each other. You can learn to rely on your opposite for a wider range of support, and you will gain confidence in your own abilities as you each expand your roles.

Questions to Consider

1. How do you consider your strengths when selecting which role to play?

2. Are you okay sharing equal credit with your partner even when you do more work on an assignment?

3. In what situations do you advocate for your opposite?

4. How do you occasionally break out of your expected roles?

5. How often do you provide on-the-spot coaching to each other?

Chapter 6

Destroy the Dislike

"We were often angry with one another. At other times we were very warm. I think we shared a strong sense of morality about films that offended us, either by their content or their general stupidity."

—Television host Roger Ebert on his
relationship with cohost Gene Siskel[27]

Destroy the Dislike: When you respect each other
and act like friends you can talk openly and have fun.

For many years, Gene Siskel and Roger Ebert were the only sources for film criticism on television. But Siskel and Ebert couldn't stand each other. When you watched them converse and give their classic "thumbs up" and "thumbs down" about that month's new releases, you were guaranteed to see sparks fly. They often disagreed, and clips of their interviews reveal a complex relationship. They bickered, laughed, and raised their voices, both on camera and off.

In one outtake, Roger, the extrovert, tells introverted Gene to "sound a little excited" and Gene tells Roger to "sound a little *less* excited."[28] It gets personal when Roger, who describes himself as not "the shy, retiring type," seems comfortable winging the intros and accuses Gene of being unable to ad lib.

In the beginning they "hardly had a single conversation," said Ebert. "We were competing critics, and for a long time we fought it out on the show before we suddenly realized that we are doing this show together. . . . This is something we are building together."[29]

Sadly, Gene Siskel died of a brain tumor in 1999, and, in an interview on *Larry King Live*,[30] a visibly upset Roger commented on how the dislike masked real mutual respect, built over years. He said, "We had all kinds of little vibes that we shared with each other. There was verbal shorthand. We had been through so many movies and experiences together that we could read each other's minds." Ebert said they both loved movies so much, especially good ones, and he recalled with affection one lovely scene when Gene crawled over to him in the dark while watching *Fargo* saying, "This is why we go to the movies."

Later he said, "I did not realize how much we actually agreed on movies. In this last year, I've missed him so much. . . . I had almost taken for granted having access to this brilliant mind."

They had their love of movies and an underlying deep respect for each other in common, even though they often fought like cats and dogs. Ebert recalls, "When we disagreed about films, Gene loved it. Because no, I'm not a shy and retiring type, so of course I pushed back, and he loved that, too. The thing that I also loved about him is he respected my opinions about the movies, and he did listen to me."

The popularity of Siskel and Ebert's reviews over the years amply demonstrated that they achieved great results from their partnership. Apparently, they made their greatest progress when they stopped competing, got over their initial contempt for each other, and focused their work on their shared audience. They reaped huge benefits from growing their friendship by destroying any early dislike they had for each other.

Why Destroying the Dislike Matters

You Get Results

In Perth, Australia, another introvert/extrovert pair demonstrates a similar dynamic. Extroverted Ron Alexander, a former national soccer star and now the director general of the Department of Sport and Recreation in that city, describes his introverted colleague Graham as "one of the world's most decent people." He says they are "kindred spirits." Each week, they have great robust conversations over coffee that have led to major changes in the direction and growth of their department. Both second-career professionals, they bonded over a desire to build capacity, make a difference, and leave a legacy. To that end, they spearheaded the building of a standalone sports and recreation complex that is one of the most respected in Australia.

In his book *Powers of Two*, author Joshua Wolf Shenk writes of numerous pairs who become friends despite being very different in temperament. One such pair of opposites Shenk describes is Steve Jobs (the extrovert) and Steve Wozniak (the introvert). He says, "They began their friendship hanging out in a friend's garage, discovering what they had in common, debating such topics as whether Bob Dylan or the Beatles were better musicians. Yet, while they shared a distinct vision, their temperaments and characters diverged sharply. Jobs could bore into people like a laser beam. . . . Wozniak described being 'scared to talk because I thought I'd say the wrong thing.' "[31]

They weren't natural friends, but building on a shared love of music and their passion for electronics, the two began working together, planting the seeds for what became the Apple computer and an actual technological revolution. They have become a classic example of the dynamic collaboration of opposites.

You Expand Your World

I met Mollie my sophomore year of high school. She was so different from my other friends. More than six feet tall with long red hair, she moved very slowly, her shoulders slumped, and she spoke few words. But she was the coolest girl I ever met. She wrote poetry, hitchhiked on the weekends, and told us she once rode on a motorcycle with Bob Dylan on a break from her summer camp.

It didn't matter whether that last fact was true. I was a "fan girl" from the start of our friendship. We played folk songs together on the guitar. She taught me to write and appreciate poetry. She laughed at my stories and seemed to find my extroverted energy and me amusing.

Like many high school friendships, ours ended and we lost touch. I saw her once a few years later on a trip to California, but I remember it being a bit awkward. We had each moved on. But what matters most is that while it lasted we each grew and shared an experience that expanded our worlds. Until I met Mollie, I never believed that I was creative. She helped me to tap into that important part of myself.

Errol la Grange, the Australian online training company founder and CEO, said that Anthony, his business partner and friend, expands his world. "I have probably spent more contact hours with Anthony than any other human. He constantly intrigues and interests me. I like spending time with him, whether that is in or out of work." He continued, "Anthony is way more process driven than I am." I tend to get bored much more easily and go seek stimulation. He has taught me to be a little more proactive and reliable in my processes. Perhaps Anthony has learned to be a bit more spontaneous. I do think that Anthony has come out of his shell more as a result of being around me." These are friends who destroyed the dislike and are expanding their worlds together.

Relationships that Change Get Results

Introvert/extrovert partners at work go through a similar trajectory of intense interaction and letting go. Some of them, like consulting partners Billie Alban and Barbara Bunker, become friends and grow closer in their later years, which benefited their consulting business. These two now travel the world together. Others, like Siskel and Ebert, move from competition and even animosity toward affection after a lifetime of work together. And still others, like Mollie and me, have a strong friendship for a finite period, learning and growing from each other and then moving on, completing our time together but not forgetting the gifts we have received.

⚠ How Destroying the Dislike Breaks Down

Shutting Down Communication

In small businesses and in large organizations alike, people become friends because they work so closely together. Extroverted Leila is an experienced dental assistant at the side of an introverted dentist-boss, Jake. They didn't always get along. His pervasive silence grated on her, and her frequent talking annoyed him.

After working together and learning to accept the alien, things switched and Leila now considers Jake a work friend. You can pick up an easy, relaxed rapport between the two. Leila explains that she can tell when something is bothering Jake not by any words but by his exasperated facial expression. When he doesn't tell her what the cause is, she is frustrated trying to figure it out. "Is it me or is it a patient?" she wonders. "It doesn't wear well on me to keep feelings inside," Leila said.

When the introverted partner shuts down, the extrovert ideally takes steps to bring him out. At a break between patients she asks her boss what the problem is, and they discuss it and then move on. When they don't have this check-in time, the office takes on the tension that hovers between them. Leila believes that destroying the dislike has allowed for their open communication flow.

When introverts and extroverts who work together don't talk, their results suffer. Songwriter Alan Jay Lerner and his partner Frederick Loewe wrote such musicals as *Camelot* and *My Fair Lady*. Author Joshua Wolf Shenk describes this sad situation. He quotes Lerner from his memoir, saying, "Too much was never said. In the end we were a little like the couple being discussed in one of Noel Coward's early plays. 'Do they fight?,' said one. 'Oh, no, said the others. They're much too unhappy to fight.'"[32]

Clearly, Lerner believed that he and his partner could have produced even more memorable music if they had communicated more. They—and we—would have benefited.

Forcing the Friendship

When I was going through a tough time with girlfriends in middle school, my mom said she believed that you needed only one really good friend. I didn't believe her at the time, but I now understand. Not everyone needs to be your friend, especially at work. Sometimes the worst damage someone can do to an emerging friendship is to force it. Eula learned that the hard way.

Eula is an extroverted salesperson at a technology company. Sophia, the introverted account manager, likes to slowly warm up to new people. When Sophia joined the company, Eula invited Sophia out to lunch and kept stopping by her work area uninvited.

Eula revealed what Sophia thought was "TMI (too much information) regarding her family problems." Guarding her own privacy, Sophia found herself distancing herself from Eula and ignoring Eula's invitations. When the time came to provide input on Eula's performance, Sophia criticized Eula's talkative, overbearing nature. What might have become a strong working relationship derailed when one partner failed to respect her partner's style and space. Unfortunately, in her running diatribe, Eula didn't slow down to notice Sophia's responses. She generated a distrustful dislike in Sophia, and by then it was too late.

Majoring in Minors—and Forgetting the Goal

Extroverted Web designer Andy and his introverted artist partner Clive have worked well together in a growing business. They became friends over six years and have received accolades for their work from several high-profile clients.

On one project things almost imploded. Their new website client called to tell Andy, who was the website fix-it guy, that the site was down. Rather than picking up the call from a client, Clive, who hates the phone, let it ring. Then he picked up the message as he usually does. Next, he emailed Andy to give him the message about the website problem. Andy fired back an angry response to Clive, asking him why he hadn't immediately jumped on the issue and called Andy.

The pair first solved the website issue, then discussed this disconnect in their communication. Clive agreed that in the future he would respond immediately to client emergencies.

Introverted colleagues tend to use written communication (text, email, social networking) when a voice-to-voice communication would be more effective. Extroverts often overuse verbal modes (Skype video, phone, coffee). Both need to have a clear understanding of which method to use in different client scenarios.

When Clive's handling of the client's emergency sidetracked the two friends, everyone lost. They had both fallen into the trap of allowing stresses in their own communication to overshadow their shared vision.

Solutions: Destroying the Dislike Can Enable Stunning Outcomes

Keep Your Vision Front and Center

The friendships of opposites are often complicated. Like Siskel and Ebert, opposites often act like children, arguing and even yelling at each other. But Siskel and Ebert's shared vision of putting on a great show kept them moving forward. It is precisely this tension that sets the stage for real creative breakthroughs.

There is no way that any close relationship can exist without strain, frustration, and the occasional eye roll. Fighting means you have a strong opinion. So share it, discuss, and engage, but remember that you and your mission are bigger than any bickering.

Get Inspired by Common Symbols

Opposites Dave Gilboa and Neil Blumenthal are cofounders and co-CEOs of the unique eyewear Web retailer Warby-Parker. According to their website, they sell "high-quality, retro-hipster eyeglasses for less than half the price of most designer specs" and donate glasses to people in developing countries, helping them to set up businesses selling glasses.[33]

The two partners selected a blue-footed booby, a bird from the Galapagos, as one of their symbols. Found in rare corners of the world, it is a quizzical-looking bird with quirky webbed feet. This symbol is shorthand in the Warby-Parker culture for their values, including "being worldly and informed, curious, constantly learning and taking your work seriously but not you seriously."[34] This symbol serves as a touchstone for these two friends and the entire company to remind them of their values. Organizations can help destroy the dislike in their genius opposites by finding unifying symbols to keep everyone focused on common values.

Be Open to Short-Term Friendships

Sometimes connections can be fleeting and still offer a chance to learn. After hearing my speech at the American Library Association on how much we can learn from having focused conversations, an introverted librarian named Beth wrote:

> *Vegas was a hard town to be in as an introvert. That night, as I hailed a cab, I was overly tired and just wanted to get to the hotel and away from the crush of people. . . . The cabbie started talking with me, something I generally avoid, but I thought about practicing "engaged listening" and decided I would try it. It turns out, we had an amazing conversation about the Nag Hammadi codices and the educational system in Nevada.*

Beth went on to say that she was grateful she took the time to listen and learn from this extroverted driver. Being open to listening and having conversations with strangers can expand your world, for both introverts and extroverts.

Balance the Need for Privacy and Freely Sharing Information

Extroverted banker Brook learned to accept introverted branch services manager Monica's need for boundaries in their relationship. Though surprised at the time, she eventually accepted Monica's decision to not share details about her wedding in workplace conversation. Doesn't every young woman want to spill those details to her women friends? Monica prefers to keep her personal life private, and when Brook realized that she backed off and gave her employee and work friend the space she wanted.

Here Is Some Advice

To the extrovert: Cool your heels and let the introverts you know share what they want to, when they do. They build trust this way. With time, introverts will reveal more and your friendship with them will settle into a comfortable rhythm of its own.

To the introvert: Share enough information so that the extroverts you know will feel like they can connect, stopping short of revealing information that makes you feel vulnerable. When they feel comfortable with you, a mutual conversation of give and take will emerge.

And both of you need to be patient.

Talk About Stuff

"The death knell to real collaboration is politeness,"[35] said biologist Francis Crick.

Just as Leila encourages her introverted dentist Jake to get his thoughts off his chest, opposites who talk about what's on their minds form deeper working relationships.

Introverted consultant Maureen said that she would have started talking about her differences with her opposite Mark earlier in their partnership if she had it to do again.

Facebook executives Mark Zuckerberg and Sheryl Sandberg are known for their closed-door meetings, where they discuss "products, strategy, deals, personnel, and each other." In discussing their friendship, Sandberg describes how she coaches Zuckerberg on his public speaking. He compliments his opposite by remarking, "We can talk for 30 seconds and have more meaning be exchanged than in a lot of meetings that I have for an hour."[36]

Think about having your conversations on neutral ground, such as inviting a guest to dinner out at a restaurant, rather than at your home. You will both be more likely to be civil to be each other when inevitable emotions flare up.

Drive Each Other a Little Nuts

Leigh Thompson, author of the *Creative Conspiracy*, was quoted in an article in *Fast Company* that made the case for opposites working together when she said, "I need to find someone who drives me nuts, but that person is going to be a good check on my behavior."[37]

Errol and Anthony joke around constantly. They laugh at each other's differences and themselves. Errol says, "Yes, Anthony pretty much always beats me at table tennis. I don't mind that too much because we always have a good laugh. What is frustrating is that he always prioritizes work over playing table tennis. SPAT!"

Once, upon returning from a break in leading a training class I found that my introverted teammate Lloyd had placed a long piece of masking tape down the middle of our table. Admittedly, I had been slowly encroaching on his side with my "stuff," and he wanted to give me a pretty obvious clue.

Traveling to so many cities together had given us this easy rapport, and the participants laughed along with us. Rather than resenting each other, we found a way to overcome a dislike for our style differences and enjoy the pranks that followed.

Comedian and pianist Victor Borge said that "laughter is the shortest distance between two people." Successful introvert/extrovert partners live that out. Reach into your natural sense of humor to laugh every day so that you can relax, support each other, and, most importantly, remain friends while you're working together.

Summary: That First Step Is the Steepest

Opposites who do the work of crafting a friendship can achieve outcomes that more like-minded teams might not reach. They can do this only if they can figure out how to act like friends and overcome any tendency to dislike each other over differences throughout the process.

Ideally, both grow. Skills that opposites need to destroy the dislike include keeping your vision front and center, getting inspired by common symbols, being open to the possibility that this might be a short-term friendship, balancing privacy and sharing, talking about stuff, and driving each other a little nuts. Look at the time you spend together as leading to possible lasting change—a change that a team of people who are not opposites probably could not have created.

Questions to Consider

1. What actions do you take toward being friendly?

2. How do you balance the needs for privacy and openness?

3. What role does laughter have in your relationship?

4. How do you show curiosity about your opposite's interests?

5. What are you learning from your opposite?

Chapter 7

Each Can't Offer Everything

"Though the two men had strikingly different tempera-
ments—Roosevelt's original and active nature at odds
with Taft's ruminative and judicial disposition—their
opposing qualities actually proved complementary,
allowing them to forge a powerful camaraderie and
rare collaboration."

—Historian Doris Kearns Goodwin on the relationship of
opposites William Howard Taft and Teddy Roosevelt[38]

Each Can't Offer Everything: Know that each one
of you is incapable of offering everything and that
for true diversity you work in concert to provide the
widest range of options to others.

Stephanie and Jane work together in a video production company. Stephanie is definitely the more introverted of the two. They both say how much their differences drive the success of their shoots and ongoing relationships with clients.

Stephanie explains, "We discovered how well our personalities work together first through our video production duties. Jane always made the client feel at ease and answered any questions while I would make sure all the equipment was fine-tuned and ready. The complementary traits continued to benefit our team as we added more tasks to our workload, such as sales and administration.

"To make our company as successful as possible, Jane and I have been able to fine-tune our division of labor in the company over the years, with a focus on our personality strengths. By using her extrovert strengths and my introvert strengths, we can be as efficient as possible and create the best quality videos for our clients. I can't imagine a better fit; together we are unstoppable."

In the eyes of the client, "unstoppable" means exemplary service from these responsive, creative service providers. They very likely don't know where Jane ends and Stephanie begins. They are receiving much more than just one-plus-one from this dynamic duo.

Why Each of You Not Offering Everything Matters

The Client Sees a Seamless Flow

When introvert/extrovert pairs are in synch, they take the time to draw from what they each naturally do best. A client of Stephanie and Jane's told me she was delighted at the impact of the team's seamless flow. "I know they have strong personality differences. But all I knew was they were a joy to work with and delivered a superb video product."

When introvert/extrovert pairs are successful, they flow in front of the client though they may differ behind the scenes. By gently stepping into their natural roles, the pair avoids competing about the best way to do things. And they end up exceeding expectations.

You Give Clients a Choice of Personalities

Mike Wittenstein, managing lead principal of a customer experience consulting firm called Storyminers, formed a partnership with Stan Phelps, founder and experience architect of 9 Inch Marketing. Mike said, "Our differences come across as a strength when we sell our team. Clients like to have personalities to pick from to match their audiences. They like to know that when they hire one of us, they get both of us."

The adage "the whole is greater than the sum of its parts" is true, especially over time and over complex projects.

The Medley Gives Clients a Range of Views

Strong introvert/extrovert pairs sidestep pressure to be on the same page and instead use their differences as a way to present diverse and even divergent opinions. There is never one right answer, so the best way to serve a client is to present the widest range of options to help them choose the best one for them. The client wins by having this array of choices.

I copresented a program to my professional organization on creating a niche in your business. My introverted French Canadian partner, Ghislaine, recounted a low-key, methodical, and planned approach to her business growth. I described a more organic and fluid way of building a company. The audience clearly benefited from the diverse perspectives we brought to the subject, as demonstrated by the vibrant discussion and high engagement.

We are in an age of collaborating with our customers. When you and your partner present various views on how to tackle a problem or offer conflicting opinions, you also encourage clients themselves to dig deeper to find their best solution. You are all in it together. Just as you wouldn't want to hire an internal team composed of people just like you, you wouldn't want to bring in an outside service provider to think exactly like you.

Introvert/extrovert partnerships give you more options to consider. And in the end, a more innovative and inclusive solution will emerge. Introverted consultant Maureen says that when she is teaching, she will give a different opinion from her extroverted colleague Mark. "We use our differences. Students see that you can be working on an issue and there is more than one way of looking at it. Our clients tell us that we are very fluid and that the dance doesn't feel artificial. You obviously work together."

Listening to customers is not just important for opposites in the business world. Creative pairs also serve a market and need to listen and respond to that market. In his book *Powers of Two*, Joshua Wolf Shenk provides many examples of creative pairs like Vincent Van Gogh (the extrovert) and his art dealer brother and champion Theo (the introvert), who did just that. Shenk writes that Theo became an adviser to Vincent, "whose early works were dark and dreary."[39] Theo urged him to pay attention to Impressionism, a movement Vincent knew nothing about until he came, finally, to join his brother in Paris in February 1886. His famous "Sunflowers" paintings are a result of listening to that sound advice from his brother and opposite.

⚠ How Each of You Can't Offer Everything Breaks Down

In offering diversity to clients, pairs who offer "two for one" can work beautifully, but can also fail memorably. Here are a few ways that failure can happen.

One Style Dominates the Partnership

One style can dominate the partnership. The introvert can spend too much time in reflection and analysis, and progress stalls. Decisions aren't forthcoming and conflicts hang in the air, waiting to be resolved. When time is of the essence, indulging the introvert's strength of analysis can prevent progress. The extrovert, on the other hand, can prematurely rush the partner or the client along in the desire to make the sale or complete a project. Their over the top follow up and push toward resolution can cause the customer to walk away.

One of the opposites can hog the spotlight, as in this example from introverted Sheri, describing her extroverted boss, Jon. "In every meeting with customers, I felt that I was the cupcake and he was the cake, even though I had more firsthand knowledge about what the issues were. It seemed as though he wanted to get the 'face time' in front of the client. It was very difficult to get my ideas heard in our prep meetings and during the actual calls. I was so frustrated and I think the customer lost out by not hearing from more knowledgeable but quieter contributors."

You Ignore Preferences (At Your Peril)

Although many people do consider personality styles when they work with clients, many opposites still don't understand or know how to apply this knowledge. With time and work pressures, we focus on the task at hand and forget to consider the introvert/extrovert angle.

Also when we communicate the way we prefer to be spoken to, not the way the other person prefers, we run into problems. For example, the extrovert forges ahead on full octane and the introvert forgets to make time for face time. Individually these acts don't amount to a great deal but over time these missed connections accumulate, leading to frustrations on both sides of the street.

You Fail to Prepare Together

We've seen the advantages to clients when introvert/extrovert partners offer true service. These teams of opposites can offer many viable choices to their clients. While a wider menu expands the range of possible offerings to customers, without adequate preparation by the opposites, the clients' heads will spin.

Brian is an introverted healthcare consultant. He decided to bring along Ava, his extroverted project manager on an important sales call with Lisa, the nursing director of a major teaching hospital. Lisa posed a question about alternative solutions to Ava, who responded verbosely in great detail. Brian observed Lisa's eyes glazing over and gently interrupted Ava to simplify the choices for his prospective client. Shortly after that he sealed the deal. Ava's input was definitely important, but without rehearsing their joint presentation and preparing their pitch and answers to potential questions, the company nearly lost a key client and major sale.

You Overlook Necessary Buy-In

Walt is an introverted public librarian who works in a Midwestern city with his extroverted boss Daniel, who is in charge of community relations. At a recent Chamber of Commerce meeting, Daniel hatched a plan with a local non-profit to co-sponsor a series of author visits and programming at the library. He presented this plan to Walt with great enthusiasm. The plan, he explained, would bring in new and old library patrons and be a major step toward the library's efforts to remain relevant.

Walt heard his boss's enthusiastic proposal and immediately felt like running the other way. Why hadn't he been asked for his input before Daniel brokered the deal? How would Walt have time to prepare for many activities and logistics? On top of this, Walt's boss told him he was expecting a "homerun." Daniel had not received the necessary buy-in from Walt before making promises to the nonprofit. Had he spent the time to partner with Walt in order to make the project a success, a great deal of anxiety and fits and starts could have been avoided.

Solutions: Use What You Know About Your Opposite; Apply It to Clients

Use I/E Preferences to Win Business

You can serve clients or customers best when you know their preferences. Author Paul Tieger calls this "speed-reading people."[40] Both of you can match your energy to your customer's approach.

Consider mirroring your introverted client's laid-back energy. Take the time to build trust and allow the client time to process new data. Are you pausing and allowing for silence? Are you addressing the process, the information, and the systems—areas that introverts lean toward? How about suggesting that introverts reflect on new information and write you an email with their response?

You can also match your extroverted customers' "out there" energy. Are you ramping up your eye contact and smiling some? How about building rapport by inquiring about their interests and family? Or consider talking out a few of your ideas so they can hear what you are thinking before the final discussion

You each can't offer everything, but both of you can tune in to your introverted and extroverted clients and adapt accordingly. Don't change who you are, but flex your style. This will allow you to be so much more effective with all of them.

Flex by Taking Practical Actions

Knowing your client's preferences allows you to check in with them to make sure you are meeting their needs. Barbara Bunker, an extroverted organizational development consultant, described a very effective activity called "The Fishbowl" that her work partner Billie Alban instituted because she was concerned that introverts like her would be talked over by the extroverts in their groups.

Billie would ask all of the introverts to move their chairs together in a circle. Then she asked the extroverts to spread out into an outer ring. As with a fishbowl, the extroverted participants watched from the outer ring, and the introverts worked in a circle facing inward. Billie then asked the introverts to share their ideas and reactions to the discussion. The introverts opened up and offered their reactions and feelings. Their comments were illuminating to the extroverts, who were enlightened by the honest disclosures that surfaced. The subsequent discussion included many more varied viewpoints after the introverts had been given permission to express their views without visual or auditory interruption.

Model Client Openness by Using Your Own Differences

When clients and customers see you embrace your own differences as opposites, you model and create a climate of openness. Clients are more likely to consider different ideas this way. They hear you and your opposite offering your own different points of view in your natural style. It inspires them to do the same.

One member of a genius pair said, "Having different ways of saying things is beneficial. . . . When we are with a client, the conversation is very fluid. We go back and forth and clients see that people with different styles can work well together. The dance in front of them doesn't feel artificial."

Don't try to hide your introvert/extrovert differences when working with clients and customers. Let them see that you can have differing perspectives as you talk things through.

Gather Information About What's Working Well and What's Not

As part of the free flow of information between you and your clients, ask them questions about what is working and what needs to be improved. Does the product or service meet their standards? Do they get timely responses from your team? What else would they like to see you offer? Are there regular enough communications with them, and do they find those effective?

You can use surveys and interviews to collect data on your customers' experience. Meet as opposites to decide what changes you plan on implementing based on their feedback. Be clear about your roles and get back to customers in a timely manner with this information. Between you and your client (and your strengths), you should be able to respond to your customers' needs. There are times, however, when neither of you can offer everything, and you or the customer decides to work with someone else or not continue the project. Strong communication between you, as opposites, will help you weather these storms.

Strengthen Your Pair's Performance

You can apply your introvert/extrovert knowledge and strengths to work better with your partner and also serve the customer.

Consider this example. Brook, the extroverted vice president/branch manager, said that her introverted employee Monica does not always approach customer situations the same way that outgoing Brook would. Monica is a top employee, but one day Brook noticed that Monica was reticent about quickly intervening with a teller who was faced with a difficult customer. Brook provided feedback to Monica about getting involved sooner, and Monica was very open to receiving it.

Monica's willingness to learn from her highly extroverted boss helps her serve the customer in the best possible way. Each partner needs to be open about giving and getting feedback so that the customer benefits from this diversity. Refer to the On-the-Spot Coaching Tips chart in Chapter 5 for guidelines.

In another example, Dick Axelrod, introverted co-author of *Let's Stop Meeting Like This*, said that listening to his wife and coauthor Emily's extroverted voice in his head helped him while he was writing his book. Dick was able to imagine the reactions of his more extroverted readers, a significant portion of his target reader base. "Emily is more like our clients. . . . I tried to keep her in mind as I was writing. I'd think, 'How can we say this in a different way?'" Imagining Emily's voice helped Dick to connect with more of their readers and no doubt has contributed to the book's success.

Get Out the Whiteboard

Much of the work on a client project or service delivery takes place behind the scenes. Introverted and extroverted partners work best when they can tease out multiple perspectives using their own unique strengths. They dip in and out of each other's skills numerous times to help the outcome be the team's best shot.

Ricky Woolverton, the extroverted sales manager, said of his introverted partner Liz, "We use each other as sounding boards. We often get away from the action and find a conference room with a whiteboard. We will list words and the pros and cons of a decision we have to make. We will even role-play different customers and employees before making our presentations in order to understand different potential viewpoints."

This deliberate whiteboard time gives them each a chance to air their concerns as well. Liz said, "I look at the data carefully and then proceed. Ricky wants to 'get it done.'"

Using a whiteboard to prepare allows them to create the best solution by using the strengths of each person's style. This approach allows the client to receive outstanding results from your combined work as opposites. Each can't do it alone.

Summary: Nurture Your Two Perspectives to Improve the Solution

In the work of opposites, offering clients introvert and extrovert perspectives not only gives the client a range of views, but may also help the client reach better solutions. Accepting that each can't offer everything requires special nurturing skills: the team of opposites needs to understand clients' introvert/extrovert preferences, check in often with clients, leverage its own differences to encourage clients to speak up, and constantly gather client feedback. The work, however, is worth the rewards. Clients often feel as though the contributions of opposites give them service above and beyond what they expected.

Questions to Consider

1. How do clients and customers benefit from your diverse and divergent opinions?

2. How do you gather information on what is and is not working with clients?

3. How do you synch up your ideas before meeting with those you serve?

4. How do you model openness to your clients?

5. How do you take steps to understand your client's introverted or extroverted energy?

Part III
The Results

Chapter 8

Keep Your Eye on the Results

"We have such different ways of seeing the world and it is magnificent!" said extroverted Olivia about working with her introverted partner Henry.

Getting to that place doesn't just happen by wanting it. Creating extraordinary results with your opposite entails a lot of frustration and confusion before the joys of shared outcomes emerge.

Keeping your relationship vital and active—not just coasting—is the goal. Just as careful synchronization can lead to strong partnerships, getting tangled in your differences can lead to disastrous outcomes.

So remember that both of you always need to keep your eye on the results and not confuse the outcome with the process. The outcome is the shared goal you are both moving toward. The process is how you both get there. With I/E opposites, it is never the same way for both people.

Throughout the course of your relationship, you should both continually come back to the big question: *"What is the common goal we want to emerge from all of this?"*

If you and your opposite can stop focusing on your differences and instead look at your common goals, you have an excellent chance of creating extraordinary results.

Now Move from Inspiration to Action

There are many moving parts in this delicate dynamic, and the recommendations made in this book will help you both move to that magnificent place Olivia describes.

Need some questions to help you get started? Here you go:

1. How can you make the five tangible steps of ABCDE from The Genius of Opposites Process accessible to you? Keep the process visible. Consider putting our downloadable version (available at www.jenniferkahnweiler.com) on your smart phone, at your desk, or on your screensaver. Make it part of your daily life.

2. Were there any particular stories or examples in the book that inspired you? What lessons are you taking from these stories or examples that apply to your own situation?

3. How can you use a different approach with your opposite? Refer to the Solutions sections in Chapters 3 through 7 and commit to one new behavior to apply each week. Notice any differences in the results you are getting.

4. Are you willing to retake the quiz in Chapter 2 in thirty days?

   - Ask your partner to retake the quiz as well.
   - Did your individual score improve?
   - How about your partner's score?
   - What is working about working together?
   - What isn't working about working together?
   - What outcomes are you now achieving?

5. Think of a current work project in which you are working with an opposite. Are there places you two are stuck? Which step in the ABCDE process can you apply to improve the situation?

6. Which of the ABCDE steps might be useful to focus on with family and friends? Trying on these tools outside of work will give you just the

practice and confidence you need to strengthen those workplace relationships and move toward outcomes.

7. Looking ahead, what are the results you want to achieve for your next assignment, project or creative endeavor? How can you apply the Genius of Opposites Process for a good start with future opposites?

As you move from inspiration to action, let's end with some wise send-offs from the two Australian partners, Errol and Anthony, whose voices you have heard throughout this book.

"*There is no way our business would have grown and become viable without each other. Notwithstanding our differences, we can both start and finish each other's sentences.*"

Errol LaGrange, Extrovert

"*We really are like yin and yang. They are different by nature and it is the difference that is the basis of the strength. From there you find the common ground, the shared values and vision, but at the core is diversity.*"

Anthony Morris, Introvert

To echo Olivia's opening quote,
I wish you spectacular outcomes as you
find your genius together.
Thank you for coming along on this journey.

Notes

Chapter 1

1. Oliver Leiber, "Opposites Attract." Recorded by Paula Abdul, 1988.
2. Beth Buelow, *The Introvert Entrepreneur: Amplify Your Strengths and Create Success on Your Own Terms* (New York: Penguin, to be released 2016).
3. "Married with Luggage," *The Introvert Entrepreneur: Episode 66*, May 15, 2014, narrated by Beth Buelow, http://theintrovertentrepreneur.com/2014/05/15/ep66 -married-with-luggage-a-conversation-with-betsy-warren- talbot/
4. Jonathan Rauch, "Caring for Your Introvert," *The Atlantic Magazine*, March 1, 2003.
5. Devora Zack, *Networking for People Who Hate Networking* (San Francisco: Berrett-Koehler, 2010).

Chapter 3

6. Joshua Wolf Shenk, *Powers of Two* (Boston: Houghton Mifflin Harcourt, 2014), 245.
7. Stephen Sondheim, "Six by Sondheim," HBO, documentary by James Lapine and Frank Rich, December 2013.
8. "Spielberg and Williams," *TCM Presents: AFI's Master Class: The Art of Collaboration*, TCM, November 2013.
9. Brad Stone, *The Everything Store* (Boston: Little, Brown, 2013), 28.

10. David Kiersey and Marilyn M. Bates, *Please Understand Me* (Prometheus Nemesis, 1984), 1.

Chapter 4

11. Joshua Wolf Shenk, *Powers of Two* (Boston: Houghton Mifflin Harcourt, 2014), 19.

12. "Dare to Disagree," *TED*, August 2012, narrated by Margaret Heffernan, www.ted.com/talks/margaret _heffernan_dare_to_disagree/transcript?language=en.

13. Betsy Polk and Maggie Ellis Chotas, *Power Through Partnership: How Women Lead Better Together* (San Francisco: Berrett-Koehler, 2014), 109.

14. Robert Lutz, "Straight Talk from Bob Lutz on 6 Auto CEOs," *Fortune*, June 4, 2013, http://fortune.com/2013/06/04/straight-talk-from-bob -lutz-on-6-auto-ceos.

15. Nilofer Merchant, "Sitting is the Smoking of our Generation," *Harvard Business Review*, January 14, 2013, https://hbr.org/2013/01/sitting-is-the-smoking-of-our -generation.

Chapter 5

16. David A. Heenan and Warren Bennis, *Co-Leaders: The Power of Great Partnerships* (New York: John Wiley, 1999), 227.

17. Peter Elstrom, "Alibaba CEO Lu Rises From Holiday Inn Job to Ma Confidant," *Bloomberg*, November 18, 2013, www.bloomberg.com/news/2013-11-17/alibaba-ceo-lu -rises-from-holiday-inn-job-to-ma-confidant-tech.html.

18. Adam Grant, "Rethinking the Extraverted Sales Ideal: The Ambivert Advantage," *Psychological Science*, April 8, 2013, 1024–1030.

19. Joshua Wolf Shenk, *Powers of Two* (Boston: Houghton Mifflin Harcourt, July 2014), 66–67.

20. David A. Heenan and Warren Bennis, *Co-Leaders: The Power of Great Partnerships* (New York: John Wiley, 1999), 279.

21. Roger Rosenblatt, "The Straight Man," *Modern Maturity*, July–August 1996, 20.

22. "The Diner," *I Love Lucy*, CBS, March 1954, www.imdb.com/video/hulu/vi3032721177.

23. Michael Patrick Welch, "An Interview with John Oates, Who Deserves Your Respect," *Vice*, October 21, 2013, www.vice.com/read/john-oates-new-orleans-interview

24. Adam Grant, *Give and Take* (New York: Viking, 2013), 79–82.

25. Nancy Ancowitz, "Secrets to a Successful Introvert-Extrovert Team," *Psychology Today*, March 15, 2010, www.psychologytoday.com/blog/self-promotion-introverts/201003/secrets-successful-introvert-extrovert-team.

26. Brad Sugars, "Avoid These 7 Partnership Killers," *Entrepreneur*, September 10, 2008, www.entrepreneur.com/article/196912.

Chapter 6

27. Gene Siskel and Roger Ebert, "Siskel & Ebert @ The David Letterman Show," *The David Letterman Show*, NBC, 1987, interview by David Letterman, www.youtube.com/watch?v=oFr4U-iFAIw

28. Gene Siskel and Roger Ebert, "Siskel & Ebert '80s Outtakes," *Siskel & Ebert,* www.youtube.com/watch?v=OkwVz_jK3gA

29. Roger Ebert, "Ebert: A 'Life' Still Being Lived, And Fully," *NPR,* September 13, 2011, www.npr.org/2011/09/13 /140437328/ebert-a-life-still-being-lived -and-fully

30. Roger Ebert, "Roger Ebert Speaks to Larry King about Gene Siskel," *Larry King Live,* CNN, November 2009, interview by Larry King, www.youtube.com/watch?v =SRErc9HJSq8

31. Joshua Wolf Shenk, *Powers of Two* (Boston: Houghton Mifflin Harcourt, 2014), 17.

32. Joshua Wolf Shenk, *Powers of Two* (Boston: Houghton Mifflin Harcourt, 2014), 182.

33. "5 Minutes with Neil Blumenthal, Co-Founder and Co-CEO, Warby Parker," *Delta Sky Magazine,* September 2014, 30.

34. Neil Blumenthal and David Gilboa, "Dynamic Duos: 5 Brilliant Business Lessons from Warby-Parker's CEOs," *Fast Company,* December 2013, www.fastcodesign.com/3016313/design-50/dynamic-duos -5-brilliant-business-lessons-from-warby-parkers-ceos

35. Joshua Wolf Shenk, *Powers of Two* (Boston: Houghton Mifflin Harcourt, 2014), 180.

36. Miguel Helft, "Mark Zuckerberg's Most Valuable Friend," *New York Times,* October 2, 2010, www.nytimes.com/2010 /10/03/business/03face.html?_r=4&

37. Leigh Thompson, *Creative Conspiracy: The New Rules of Breakthrough Collaboration* (Boston: Harvard Business Review Press, 2013), 91.

Chapter 7

38. Doris Kearns Goodwin, *The Bully Pulpit* (New York: Simon & Schuster, 2014), 94.

39. Joshua Wolf Shenk, *Powers of Two* (Boston: Houghton Mifflin Harcourt, July 2014), 74–75.

40. Paul Tieger, *The Art of Speedreading People* (Boston: Little, Brown, 1999).

Acknowledgments

I thank my mom (Lucille Boretz) for your warmth, independence, contagious laughs, and showing me how to give and receive love. I also owe so much to my late dad (Alvin Boretz), whose vibrant energy I still feel. Though I miss you each day, your words, "Make a contribution, Jenna" guide me on this life's journey. You taught me how to be infinitely curious and tenacious.

Thank you, Bill, my husband and opposite, for loving me these many years. I know you enjoyed the coveted gift of solitude when I was holed up in my writing room. Arlo has his Alice, but I have my Bill. Keep cooking, please. I also love that you have taken on the role of the playful grandfather, "Grumps," with such natural ease.

And to you my beautiful daughters. Thank you, Lindsey Goldberg. I am so proud of how you navigate the delicate balance of being a mom and working professional while practicing self-care. You are a wise listener who truly cares about my day. Thank you, Jessie Kahnweiler. I am humbled and inspired by the beautiful, brave, and hysterical work you fearlessly put out into the world. You have helped me to trust my creative gifts.

Thank you to my beautiful granddaughter, Ava Ruth. On camera and in person, you bring me indescribable joy. I love turning the pages of books with you, and being present with you is effortless. To my son-in-law, Adam Goldberg (aka Ryan Phillipe), thank you for your wisdom, wit, and beautiful family photographs Much love and deep gratitude to my father-in-law, Lou Kahnweiler, my dear sister, Carrie Boretz, my aunt, Arline Garson, and my New York and Chicago families.

Thank you to my team. Arlene Cohn, Nick Alter, Stephen Burton, and Becky Robinson and her peeps at Weaving Influence, as well as the stellar staff at the UPS Store in Dunwoody, Georgia. I love collaborating and creating with you all. My talented editor, Nancy Breuer, is a genius with the English language and gently guided me toward crisper writing while honoring my voice and my schedule. Thank you to Jon Peck for breathing visual life into these words..

A quiet bow to Jeevan Sivasubramaniam, my brilliant Berrett-Koehler editor and genius opposite. You have helped me to reveal this book's heart and tell a deeper story. You responded to every request (even the anxious ones) with respect and patience.

Thank you, Steve Piersanti, CEO of Berrett-Koehler, for extending your hand and believing that a world that works for all values both introverts and extroverts.

I also want to acknowledge the sharp suggestions made by manuscript reviewers, Carol Metzker, Pamela Gordon, and Danielle L. Goodman. You ladies rock.

Deep appreciation goes out to other stellar members of the Berrett-Koehler community. There are none better than Kristen Frantz, Lasell Whipple, Rick Wilson, Courtney Schonfeld, Mike Crowley, Katie Sheehan, Johanna Vondeling, Maria Jesus Aguilo, Catherine Legronne, Zoe Mackey, Anna Leinberger, Grace Miller, Marina Cook, David Marshall, and Charlotte Ashlock. I will be your "queen for a day" any time!

Bows of gratitude to Elissa Amerson, Dave Basarab, Barbara McAfee, Jesse Stoner, Bill Stainton, Joshua Wolf Shenk, Adam Grant, Dick Axelrod, Emily Axelrod, Marcia Reynolds, Bill Treasurer, Susan Zeidman, Dave Summers, Alexandra Watkins, Lisa McLeod, Vinay Kumar, Michael Prince, Lan Bercu, Ken Futch, Pete Weissman, David Greenberg, Gene Greissman, Stephanie Roemer, Suzanne Richards, and Richar Ruiz for your belief in my work.

A special shout out to an incredibly giving group of authors producing groundbreaking work in the introverted space, including Susan Cain, Beth Buelow, Sophia Dembling, Nancy Ancowitz, and Val Nelson.

I am also so thankful to the readers of my books who have have opened the door to new research questions. Thank you also to the many genius opposites who openly shared your stories in hours of interviews. You were beyond generous with your time, honesty, and insights. Without you there would be no book.

There isn't room to list the many other individuals who have your imprint on this work. Thank you.

Finally, my greatest recent lessons about courage and grace have come from my fellow Berrett-Koehler author and friend, Jamie Showkeir, who is bravely facing ALS (Lou Gehrig's disease). He and his wife, Maren, are beautiful people climbing daily mountains. They are teaching me to relish each day.

Namaste.

Index

About Jennifer

 **Jennifer B. Kahnweiler, PhD, CSP** is an author, global speaker, and thought leader hailed as a "champion for introverts." Her bestselling books *The Introverted Leader: Building on Your Quiet Strength* and *Quiet Influence: The Introvert's Guide to Making a Difference* have achieved widespread appeal and have been translated into fourteen languages including Chinese and Spanish.

Her career includes jobs as an elementary school counselor, university administrator, federal government program director, and career coach. She deepened her knowledge and appreciation for introverts through her work as a learning and development professional in leading organizations such as General Electric, FreddieMac, NASA, Turner Broadcasting, and the US Centers for Disease Control.

Jennifer has delivered keynote speeches and seminars around the world, including in Australia, Vietnam, Japan, the Netherlands, and Paraguay. Her presentations include her characteristic humor, poignant stories, and practical tools. She has also been featured in *Fortune, Forbes, Time Magazine, Bloomberg Business Week,* and the *Wall Street Journal.*

She received her PhD in counseling and organizational development from Florida State University (go Seminoles!) and her earlier degrees in sociology and counseling from Washington University, St. Louis. She is a Certified Speaking Professional (CSP), a designation held by a small percentage of professional speakers. Jennifer has also served on the boards of the Berrett-Koehler Author's Co-op, the Global Task Force, and the National Speakers Association of Georgia.

Jennifer grew up outside New York City and lives with her husband, Bill, and Fred the cat (who still prefers Bill) in Atlanta, Georgia.

Working with the Author

Programs Offered by Jennifer

"Jennifer does a wonderful job by working to understand her audience and leveraging that understanding to their advantage. She gets wonderful reviews on the quality of her message and style of delivery. We look forward to bringing her back on a regular basis!"

—Suzanne Richards, Vice President, Freddie Mac

Jennifer B. Kahnweiler, PhD, CSP, is a global speaker and author who helps introverts lead with quiet confidence and organizations get the best out of their introverted talent. Her bestselling books, *The Introverted Leader: Building on Your Quiet Strength* and *Quiet Influence: The Introvert's Guide to Making a Difference*, have sold more than sixty thousand copies and have been translated into fourteen languages. These books are the basis for engaging keynote speeches, content-rich seminars, and results-driven group coaching.

Keynote Speeches

The Genius of Opposites: Creating Extraordinary Results Together

Do you often get frustrated with the introverts or extroverts in your world? It's true—opposites attract, but their success depends on how they interact. Without careful maintenance

maintenance and balance they quickly go off the rails. In this keynote, you will learn how to turn frustration into an incredible collaboration that yields long lasting results.

Based on her extensive research and experience, Jennifer will walk you through a framework called The Genius of Opposites Process. Learn to apply the five essential steps necessary for success: Accept the Alien, Bring on the Battles, Cast the Character, Destroy the Dislike, and Each Can't Offer Everything.

Quiet Influence: The New Wave of Leadership

Did you know that introverts have the most influence when they stop acting like extroverts and rely on their natural strengths? Learn how to implement the Quiet Influence Process and make the most of six natural strengths such as taking quiet time, engaged listening, and a thoughtful use of social media. Both introverts and extroverts will learn practical strategies for making the difference they were intended to make.

The Introverted Leader: Building on Your Quiet Strength

Did you know that introverts often make the best leaders? Jennifer draws upon stories and research to demonstrate how introverts can succeed as leaders and work with, not against, who they are. You will learn about the characteristics of introverts and how to use the 4 P's Process (Prepare, Presence, Push, and Practice) to manage and lead as an introverted. Successfully. You will understand why our organizations can't afford to miss out on the invaluable contributions of their quieter employees.

See her speaking demo video to learn more about her content and approach.

https://www.youtube.com/watch?v=pcojuaoMGRY

Seminars

Jennifer's content-rich half- and full-day seminars take a deeper dive into a wide range of introverted and extroverted leadership strategies. They expand on practical tools and principles drawn from her books on genius opposites, quiet influence, and introverted leadership. Sample titles include Coaching on the Fly, Engaged Listening, and Networking for Introverts and Extroverts.

All seminars are customized to your organization's needs and are highly interactive. They use proven adult learning approaches so that participants retain and apply information. They are typically delivered to leaders, emerging leaders, and professionals across their organizations. Modules include self-assessments, workbooks, case studies, and role-plays.

Group Coaching

Group coaching helps the keynote or seminar's messages "stick" in a lasting and meaningful way. Both introverted and extroverted participants gain value by addressing provocative questions stimulated by Jennifer's keynotes and seminars. These small, extended post-session coaching groups are offered via phone to give participants an opportunity to engage in focused conversations and problem solving. This allows participants to share successes, present challenges, receive peer feedback, and create action plans in a safe environment.

Follow Up on Demand Learning Programs

Jennifer's updated work can be found on an increasing number of learning platforms and mobile applications. These include Audvisor, Avanoo, G5, The Mobile Business Academy, O'Reilly.com, PDU's2Go, and Skillsoft. Check for updated program links on her website:

www.jenniferkahnweiler.com.

For More Resources

Subscribe to Jennifer's blog:

http://jenniferkahnweiler.com/blog/

And sign up for her monthly email alerts with practical tips, and access free articles and assessments at jennifer-kahnweiler.com. You can also engage with her and her community on Twitter (@jennkahnweiler), Facebook (The Introverted Leader), Linked In (Jennifer Kahnweiler), and Instagram (jkahnweiler).

Also by Jennifer Kahnweiler

Quiet Influence
The Introvert's Guide to Making a Difference

Introverts may feel powerless in a world where extroverts seem to rule, but there's more than one way to have some sway. Jennifer Kahnweiler proves introverts can be highly effective influencers when, instead of trying to act like extroverts, they use their natural strengths. Kahnweiler identifies six unique strengths introverts have and includes a Quiet Influence Quotient quiz to measure how well you're using these six strengths now. Then, through questions, tools, exercises, and real-world examples, she helps you increase your mastery of these strengths.

"This extraordinary book shows that you don't have to raise your volume to have a voice."

—Susan Cain, author of *Quiet: The Power of Introverts in a World That Can't Stop Talking*

Paperback, 192 pages, ISBN 978-1-60994-562-6
PDF ebook, ISBN 978-1-60994-563-3

BK Berrett–Koehler Publishers, Inc.
www.bkconnection.com   800.929.2929

Berrett–Koehler
Publishers

Berrett-Koehler is an independent publisher dedicated to an ambitious mission: *connecting people and ideas to create a world that works for all.*

We believe that to truly create a better world, action is needed at all levels—individual, organizational, and societal. At the individual level, our publications help people align their lives with their values and with their aspirations for a better world. At the organizational level, our publications promote progressive leadership and management practices, socially responsible approaches to business, and humane and effective organizations. At the societal level, our publications advance social and economic justice, shared prosperity, sustainability, and new solutions to national and global issues.

A major theme of our publications is "Opening Up New Space." Berrett-Koehler titles challenge conventional thinking, introduce new ideas, and foster positive change. Their common quest is changing the underlying beliefs, mindsets, institutions, and structures that keep generating the same cycles of problems, no matter who our leaders are or what improvement programs we adopt.

We strive to practice what we preach—to operate our publishing company in line with the ideas in our books. At the core of our approach is stewardship, which we define as a deep sense of responsibility to administer the company for the benefit of all of our "stakeholder" groups: authors, customers, employees, investors, service providers, and the communities and environment around us.

We are grateful to the thousands of readers, authors, and other friends of the company who consider themselves to be part of the "BK Community." We hope that you, too, will join us in our mission.

A BK Business Book

This book is part of our BK Business series. BK Business titles pioneer new and progressive leadership and management practices in all types of public, private, and nonprofit organizations. They promote socially responsible approaches to business, innovative organizational change methods, and more humane and effective organizations.

Berrett–Koehler
Publishers

Connecting people and ideas
to create a world that works for all

Dear Reader,

Thank you for picking up this book and joining our worldwide community of Berrett-Koehler readers. We share ideas that bring positive change into people's lives, organizations, and society.

To welcome you, we'd like to offer you a free e-book. You can pick from among twelve of our bestselling books by entering the promotional code **BKP92E** here: http://www.bkconnection.com/welcome.

When you claim your free e-book, we'll also send you a copy of our e-newsletter, the *BK Communiqué*. Although you're free to unsubscribe, there are many benefits to sticking around. In every issue of our newsletter you'll find

• A free e-book
• Tips from famous authors
• Discounts on spotlight titles
• Hilarious insider publishing news
• A chance to win a prize for answering a riddle

Best of all, our readers tell us, "Your newsletter is the only one I actually read." So claim your gift today, and please stay in touch!

Sincerely,

Charlotte Ashlock
Steward of the BK Website

Questions? Comments? Contact me at bkcommunity@bkpub.com.

MIX
From responsible
sources
FSC® C113845

Certified
B Corporation
bcorporation.net